# THE MOST VALUABLE MAN

## A PRIESTHOOD LEADER AT HOME

# GEORGE DURRANT

Published & Distributed by:

Granite Publishing & Distribution, LLC
868 North 1430 West
Orem, UT 84057
801-229-9023    Toll Free 1-800-574-5779
Fax 801-229-1924
www.granitebooks.com

Cover Design By: Adam Riggs
Page Layout and Design By: Michelle L. Elias

ISBN:  978-1-59936-060-7
Library of Congress Control Number: 2010926673
First Printing May 2010
10 9 8 7 6 5 4 3 2 1

**Printed in the United States of America**

Dedicated to my Bishop, Steven Webber, who encouraged me to begin this book and to his wife Janna who helped me to finish it when I had become a bit weary

# CONTENTS

## PART I

### BEING A PRIESTHOOD LEADER IN YOUR FAMILY

## PART II

### TEMPLE ORDINANCES AND COVENANTS BECOME THE FOUNDATION OF YOUR PRIESTHOOD LEADERSHIP

# PART III

## THE GOAL IS IN SIGHT

# PART I

# BEING A PRIESTHOOD LEADER IN YOUR FAMILY

# CHAPTER 1
## BEING A PRIESTHOOD LEADER IN YOUR HOME

I'm George Durrant and I would like to talk about you being a priesthood leader in your family. My friend, Robert Bryson, told me this:

"While I was at General Conference a few years ago, I walked over to the Relief Society Building. As I approached the room where the displays were, a sister distributing handouts asked me, 'Are you a priesthood leader?' I paused to consider her profound question, and then I replied, 'I believe you would have to ask my wife and children to answer that question. They are the ones who know.'"

Brother Bryson felt that the people who really knew whether or not he was a priesthood leader were his wife and children. Because he knew that the most important priesthood leadership is at home with the family.

Years ago Priesthood Meeting and Sunday School were held on Sunday morning and then Sacrament Meeting was in the early evening.

One Sunday afternoon, I was with my family in the back yard talking and eating homemade ice cream. It was nearing the time when we were to get ready to go to Sacrament Meeting. My eight year old son said, with a pained tone in his voice, "We were at church all morning. Do you want us all to go back to church again tonight?"

"Yes." I replied.

"Why?" he asked a bit defiantly.

I quietly took time to consider his question so that I could give a good reply.

My daughter, Kathryn, who was six years old, did not
need time to think. She answered, "Because Dad is a priesthood
man. That's why."

I have not always succeeded in living up to my daughter's
lofty evaluation of me but through the years, I have never quit
trying to be a priesthood man and more importantly a priesthood
leader in my home.

## PRIESTHOOD LEADERSHIP AT HOME

This book is not about you being a good elder's quorum
president, or bishop, or stake president. It is about something
more important. It is about you being a priesthood leader in your
home with your family. Priesthood leadership over at the church
is important, but priesthood leadership in the family is vital.

## GIVE YOUR FAMILY THE BEST

When I met Marilyn and fell in love with her, I felt she
deserved the best. So I asked her to marry me. Seriously, I knew
I didn't have to be handsome or rich to give her the best, I just
had to be a priesthood man.

As our eight children have become part of our family, I
felt they deserved the best. I knew that to give them the best I did
not have to be rich or famous; I just had to be a priesthood man
and lead the family in a priesthood manner.

The best a father can give his family is to help them know
they are children of God, they have divine potential, an unlim-
ited destiny, and are loved more than could ever be expressed.
You as a priesthood leader in the home along with your wife can
bring these blessings to them.

## THE HONOR OF BEING A HUSBAND AND FATHER

I was the youngest of nine children—the baby. In many
ways being the last child is a favorable position in a family. But
when I grew up I did not have what my older siblings had; I did
not have any little brothers or sisters. My friend had six younger

siblings. I was jealous of him. I wanted to grow up and have a wife and a house full of little children.

When Marilyn agreed to marry me it was the happiest day of my life, and when we had our first child I wanted to light a new star in the sky to announce our good news.

The most important item on my resume is my role as husband and father. I once filled out an information form for my employer. One of the questions was, "During your life, what honors have you received?" I skipped the question, as you are supposed to do on a test when you come to a hard one.

When I had completed all the other questions, I came back to the one that asked, "What honors have you received?" Not being able to recall any significant honors, I decided to leave the question unanswered.

I folded up the paper so it would fit into an envelope. Just as I was about to seal it, I had an impression to go back and look at the question again. I smoothed out the paper and read, "What honors have you received?" I picked up my pen and wrote, "I am a husband. I am a father." I folded up the paper, put it in the envelope and sealed it. I felt good about what I had written. For I knew then, there are no greater honors for a man than of being a husband and a father.

I hope with all my heart that you share that same feeling about your role as a husband and father. Such a feeling is the beginning of you being a priesthood man and a priesthood leader in your family

# CHAPTER 2
## BEGIN WITH THE END IN MIND

—————————————————————————

## MISSION STATEMENT

Several years ago Donald Smurthwaite wrote a magnificent book titled, A Fine Old High Priest. I liked that title because it summed up the feelings I had as a young elder, husband and father. I wanted to live every day in a way that I could eventually become a fine old high priest.

## BECOMING A FINE OLD HIGH PRIEST

I became a Branch President at the age of 30 and the Stake President felt that I should be a High Priest. I was a young High Priest, but I was not a "Fine Old High Priest" because of the "old" factor and many other factors that make a man a fine old high priest, had not yet kicked in.

Being a fine old High Priest is like a mathematics equation that goes like this:

*Ordination + endowment + integrity + temple marriage + children + grandchildren + leading a family + striving to be good + being nice + time = A Fine Old High Priest.*

I hope in my obituary it will say, "George was a Fine Old High Priest." Here are some other things that I hope will be in my obituary. "George became a Deacon at age twelve, a Teacher at age fourteen, and a Priest at age sixteen. He became an Elder at age nineteen. He became a husband, and the priesthood leader of his family in the Salt Lake Temple, at age twenty four. He became a father at age 25 and 27 and 29 and 31 and 33 and 35 and 37 and 41."

But obituaries cost a fortune these days, so cut everything else out and just say, "George was born October 20, 1931 and died??? During his lifetime he so lived that he became a Fine Old High Priest." That short sentence, "He became a Fine Old High Priest," would say everything about me that really matters.

## BEING A PRIESTHOOD LEADER BOTH AT CHURCH AND AT HOME

I have loved every calling I ever had in the church. The best part of fulfilling my church callings was that that service charged me with the priesthood power that I needed to lead my family at home. Priesthood leadership at church and priesthood leadership in the home are like the words of a song, "Love and Marriage. They go together like a horse and carriage. You can't have one without the other."

In other words, you can't spend all your time at church and neglect your family, and you can't spend all your time at home and neglect the church. You have to have both halves of service or you will lose your priesthood power.

Through the years, the most meaningful and tender spiritual times I had with my family were right after I came home from an inspiring church meeting or from doing acts of church service. And on the other hand, the most inspiring talks I ever gave at church were those I prepared while doing the dishes at home.

## THE COURAGE TO BE A HUSBAND AND FATHER

The priesthood gives me courage to embrace the future and know that the Lord has been with me in the past, and he will not desert me in the future.

I met a man once who was terrified by the fact that his wife was soon to have a baby and that he would become a father. He had been very successful in business, but he just didn't think he had what it took to be a father. I on the other hand, could not wait to be a father. I knew that with the power of the priesthood I could succeed as a father.

Consider now and forever what you can do as a husband and father as you honor your priesthood. Decide to serve in the church, serve in your family, and lead in both places in righteousness. Lead in the name of Jesus Christ. Serve with the power of the priesthood. Begin with the end in mind. Live each day of your life so that in the end your family will say of you, "Every thing he did in life, especially what he did as our husband and father caused him to become a Fine Old High Priest."

# CHAPTER 3
## Your Most Important Decision

## The Choice Is Yours

It is amazing to me what a man can do when he decides what he wants to do and he promises that he will. You must decide whether or not you want to go down the priesthood path of life that will result in you becoming a "Fine Old High Priest." If you decide to be a priesthood man and the priesthood leader in your family you can do it.

## There Are Many Paths

As you stand at the crossroads of life, you see that there are numerous paths which are in plain sight. Some are obviously paths of wickedness and corruption. You won't choose those paths because you are a good man. But there are some attractive paths that many good people have chosen; Paths that society has marked as the way to success and happiness. Some of these other paths are made to seem quite desirable by the fashions and thinking of our general society. You could easily choose such a path.

The first step in providing priesthood leadership in the family is to choose, from all the paths that people are following, the path the Lord has set. You are free to make the choice to follow the Lord's path or to follow some other path.

## CHANGING PATHS

It is far better, while you are young, to choose the path the Lord has established. However, it is never too late to leave the path you are on and move over to the Lord's path.

I recall a story of a man who came to the 40th reunion of his graduating class. He and his classmates were from a small high school. During the program each classmate spoke briefly to the others; this is what this man said:

"I have not seen many of you since our graduation some 40 years ago. I wanted to come to past reunions, but in the years after graduation, I made some choices that put me on a path of life that is quite different from the path that most of you have followed. Just a year ago I began to wonder about the path that I was on. I questioned just where I was headed. I considered how it would be to change paths and get on the path that would be a better way of life. Anyway, to make a long story short, I changed paths. I went back to church and then to the temple. I changed my lifestyle. When I learned about this reunion I decided to come. I finally felt comfortable in coming. I'm now on the same path that you are on. I feel good about it. I feel like I have come home. But I want you to know something, that other path isn't so bad, it's just that I'm not quite sure where that other path was leading me."

This man was right. Some paths seem desirable, but we usually have a sense that the alternative path is really wrong or at least it isn't quite right.

## ON THE LORD'S PATH

I'm sure you have known some men in your day of which you could say, "That man is a whole hearted priesthood man and he is truly a priesthood leader in his family." I knew such a man. His name was Tom Bean. Tom has passed on now. Through his long life he so lived that he became a Fine Old High Priest.

Tom Bean was a humble man. I used to praise him because he was so generous, inspiring, dependable, and wise in the way that he lived his life and the way he led his family. When

I would glowingly tell him of my high opinion of him, he would look down, shuffle his feet and answer, "I'm not such a much." But he was wrong in that because everyone who knew him knew that Tom Bean was "such a much." He was "such a much" because he had chosen, in his younger years, to be a priesthood man. His feelings about the priesthood flavored all that he did in every aspect of his life—especially in his relationship with his beloved Deanna and their children.

I do not know exactly when Tom decided to be a priesthood man. Perhaps it was in high school. Maybe it was when he was called on a mission. Maybe it was when he was endowed in the temple. Maybe it was during his mission. Maybe it was when he met Deanna after his mission and when the two of them merged their paths by being married in the temple. Maybe it was when he and she had their first child. All I know is that there was a time when Tom Bean decided that he would be a priesthood man. That he would not halt between two opinions or two paths. He would only have one opinion, and one path, he would serve the Lord in his personal and family life and he would lead his family to do the same.

## Many Good Men

I like to observe the fathers of the young families in our ward. Almost all of them attend church regularly. They are all gifted in many ways. It is a joy for me to know each one. They are all equally "good" as far as I can discern. However, there are some who are different, and they impress me deeply in quiet and wonderful ways. These are the ones I can tell, at some time, made a decision to be a priesthood man. I don't know when it was, but I can tell that they, like Tom Bean, no longer halt between two opinions. They are committed with all their hearts to being on the Lord's side. I stand in awe of these young men.

None of them are perfect (just ask each one's wife), but each one wishes that he could be perfect. If I could give the details of the acts of these men, it would be as inspiring as the accounts of the great priesthood men in the scriptures. When I watch these husbands and fathers as they relate to their wives and their children and to the Lord, I find myself hoping that I'm worthy to stand with these men—these priesthood men.

## Not Fully On The Lord's Path

There are other men who are honorable and good, but there is something lacking in their spiritual lives. They are not quite valiant in following the teachings of the Lord. They often leave the Lord's path. Their lives have shifted a bit to the side of the center. They have lost a portion or all of their priesthood power. They attend church. Some have been to the temple and made covenants, but they attend the temple so seldom that they can't fully remember just what covenants they made there. Many of them are good husbands and fathers. They often have callings in the Church that they do quite well, but they feel they are not fully qualified to lead their family along the path of life in a devoted manner. They are not "whole hearted priesthood men."

The good news is that there is still time. A decision to be a priesthood man awaits each of them. Who knows when it will happen? Hopefully this "mighty change" will come sooner rather than later. Nothing they could do in their lives would be more important to their wives and their children than to decide to be priesthood men and decide to make the temple ordinances and covenants the foundation of their lives and of their family leadership.

Now is the time for you as a good priesthood man to come to the aid of your family by deciding to lead them along the path the Lord has revealed. If you are on the wrong path, there is an on off ramp right there, and just ahead is an on ramp to the Lord's path. Decide now to get off the wrong path and enter the right path. That will be the most important decision you will ever make. You can do it, and doing so will make all the difference.

# CHAPTER 4
## If It Is To Be It Is Up To You

———————————————————

Now I would like to talk to you as a priesthood man. Perhaps I qualify on the grounds that I want to be on the Lord's path. Let me tell you how I decided to strive to be a priesthood man.

### My Challenges In Choosing A Path

In high school I sort of halted between two opinions or paths. I went to church each Sunday because I did not feel welcome by my mother at the Sunday dinner table if I had not done so. In the days of my youth, I wanted to be on a path where I could be known as "tough" but my mother wanted me on a path that would make me known as "a sissy." I did not know which path I really wanted to choose. I wanted to be goofy and get my friends to laugh, but I also wanted to bless the sacrament in a sincere manner.

In college I still could not fully choose a path. I wanted to get good grades, but at the same time, I would rather play ball in the gym than go to the classroom or to the library. I wanted to be popular with the girls, but I was shallow in all my relationships. I wanted to feel like I was a good guy with a good personality, but I was not dependable.

### Finding My Way

Then there came a time that things began to slowly change for me.

My closest friends from my hometown quit college and with their departure, I was a lone man on campus. I became friends with Clive Jorgenson. At first, he was a bit like me in his casual approach to college life, but then he gained an interest in Zoology and became a great student. He no longer wanted to chase girls as much as he wanted to chase insects.

In my loneliness, and with Clive's example, I decided to get serious about school. I left my seat in the back of the classroom and came down to a seat in the front. Everything seemed different from the front. I took notes. I made serious and thoughtful comments which added to the class discussion and I visited my professors in their offices.

I became interested in art and took art classes. I found myself almost running to class. I say all this because a decision to be a priesthood man cannot be made when almost all other aspects of your life are like a train wreck.

With my new found direction I decided to go on a mission. I went to the temple and was endowed. I was called to the British Mission. There I became the greatest average missionary the Church has ever had. I found out for myself that the Church was true and I determined that I should invest myself in the work with all my heart. I was never an Assistant to the mission president, but I could tell I was the Mission President's favorite.

I came home and I courted Marilyn, fell in love with her and asked her to marry me. My greatest desire was to give her the best, by being a priesthood man. We were married in the temple and I was so glad to merge my path with hers. I wanted to be with her forever. I wanted to become a father; I wanted to be a priesthood leader in my family. I attended the temple regularly and more fully understood what I was taught there. I was enlivened with the desire to keep my temple covenants.

## YOUR DECISION

Thus you can see that my decision to be a priesthood man was a long, evolutionary process. What about your decision to be a priesthood man? How did it happen? Or has it yet? Perhaps you love the Church, but not with all your heart. Perhaps you are there at church, but are not quite willing to be totally dependable, nor entirely dedicated because you have other interests that are equally or more important to you.

Perhaps you have interests outside your home that often take precedence over the needs of your wife and children. Perhaps you hesitate for one or more personal reasons to gently lead and teach your family.

## RENEWING YOUR DECISION

The decision to be a priesthood man is not something you and I do once and that is it forever. It is a decision that we need to renew each day. It is a decision that requires a heartfelt partaking of the sacrament each week. It is a decision to attend the temple and recommit again to temple covenants.

## DO WHAT PRIESTHOOD MEN DO

Once I decided to be a priesthood man I started to seek out ways to do what priesthood men do and it all began at home. As a young newlywed I loved going to college classes, but my greatest joy was in coming home. I loved to come to our little apartment in Provo and see Marilyn. I was far from perfect in my ways, yet I longed to be perfect and that longing was the very basis of my wanting to be a priesthood man.

The reason I wanted to be a priesthood man was that I was in part already a priesthood man. I wanted to do better because wanting to do better are the truest feelings of a priesthood man. That longing to do good, to be a good husband, a good father, a good friend and a good church member are the longings of a priesthood man. He is never fully where he wants to be, but with all his heart he desires to get there.

As a young husband and father I was so excited to give a talk, or to teach a class or to give a blessing or to say a kind word. I loved to attend church meetings. I felt tithing was my best investment. I loved to serve in small leadership positions. I was almost giddy about the love I felt in my heart for the Church. I know you are not like me in your emotions; I live a lot out of my heart. I get excited about the gospel and life. You may not show your feelings as I do, but you feel it just as I do. None of us are any better than the next man, but we can all feel love for the Lord. Each of us can want to honor Him by wanting to be a priesthood man, and thus we can each, even without being perfect, be a priesthood leader in our family.

## THE BLESSINGS ARE IN THE CENTER OF THE CHURCH

No matter what your present age is, there is so much of your life left to live. It is up to you to be or not to be a priesthood man.

As a new freshman in college I had one foot in my education and one foot out. In high school I always sat at the back of the classroom. I would slump down in my seat and almost disappear. I carried those same habits into my college experience. After the first semester of such disinterest I didn't have the courage to look at my grades. Finally I did look, and as I did I heard a voice from inside myself saying, "George, you can do better than that."

I put my grades in my pocket and walked over to the library. It was a nice place. I wondered why I had never gone there before. I went to class and saw a seat at the back of the room. That was the seat for me. I went toward that seat and I was about to sit down when I looked to the front of the room and saw an empty chair. I began to sit in the chair at the back, but I could still see the chair in the front. I paused. Then I made a decision that changed my entire education. I decided to go to the front and sit. Everything was different up front. I was as the center of all that was taking place. I could see better, I could hear better and class time seemed more interesting and even shorter. My education took on new meaning.

That day I became a student for the first time. I never sat in the back again. Sometimes the front seats were all taken and I had to sit in the back, but it was where my mind and body were that mattered, and they were down front. I was involved. I was not on the edge. I was in the center. So it is with the gospel.

Just remember this, there are very few of the Lord's precious blessings out on the periphery of the Church. You have to be all the way into the center of the gospel in order to feel the sweet blessings the Lord has for those who love him.

Among these blessings is the strength that the Lord will give you that will make you able to give your whole heart and soul to your family and to the Lord. As you move toward the center of the Church, you will find that the center is mostly found at home and with your family. Get all the way on the Lord's path. Don't explore other paths. You are never too far along in life to decide to dedicate your whole life to being a priesthood man, and to being a priesthood leader in your home. You can be like Tom Bean. You can live so that your wife and children will know where your heart is. Your family will know that you are striving to be the manner of man that Jesus Christ was. They will know that they can count on you. They will know that you are worthy. And when they praise you, you will say, "I'm not such a much."

However, your wife and children and grandchildren and those closest to you will know that you are "such as much" that you are a whole hearted priesthood man. You will be your family's hero. You are their priesthood leader forever. Then and only then will you be a Fine Old High Priest.

# CHAPTER 5
## YOU HAVE TO LOVE IT OR YOU CAN'T DO IT

To make a decision to become a Fine Old High priest is a beginning, but the journey is long. Only by loving your family and the gospel with all your heart will you have the endurance to continue to what you have decided to do.

### FALLING IN LOVE WITH THE CHURCH

Perhaps you feel the Church is a good part of your life. You enjoy the fellowship between you and the other members of the Church. You feel the church way of life is good for your family, but you can't say that you love the gospel with all your heart. You feel gospel living is important, but not really your highest priority. You wish you were more dedicated, but you feel you just can't find such feelings. You wonder, "How can I really get a more intense feeling about the Church, about the Lord, about the gospel?"

### IT IS A BIT LIKE FALLING IN LOVE WITH YOUR WIFE

Let me try to answer that question with some of my experiences. I feel that you and I can fall in love with the Lord a bit like we fell in love with our wives. I know that each of us and our romances with our wives have different situations and circumstances yet the inward feelings we all have are much the same. Here is what I mean:

Marilyn (Sister Burnham) and I (Elder Durrant) were young missionaries together in England. We were in the same area, Yorkshire England, for our entire mission.

Over the year and one-half that she was there, I gradually came to know her. I observed and admired her talent for teaching. (She could teach far better than me.) I observed her dedication. (She worked harder than me.) I liked her knowledge and reasoning. (She was far more bright and wise than me.) I liked the way she was organized. (She was far more organized than me.) I was impressed with the power of her testimony. (I longed to have such power.) I was hopeful that others would think as well of me as they did her. I was overwhelmed at the number of people who came to the waters of baptism through her and her companion's efforts. I loved the way she connected her work to the powers of heaven.

After observing her virtues for more than a year I was deeply impressed with all that she was. One day in the city of Hull, England, my companion and I, and Sister Burnham and her companion, were riding our bikes home from a district meeting when something happened that changed my life forever. That event was as follows:

In England, in those days, there were very few cars, so almost everyone, including missionaries, rode bikes on the roadways. Thus, we four missionaries were surrounded on all sides, by others on their bikes, as we rode along the crowded roadway. Suddenly, a few yards in front of us, a draw bridge rose so that the small ships in the river could pass. My companion and Sister Burnham's companion entered the bridge area just in time to cross before the bridge ascended. Sister Burnham and I, along with a hundred or more other bikers, were abruptly stopped.

We were waiting for about ten minutes while our companions waited on the other side of the bridge. During this time Sister Burnham and I started to talk. Our conversation went a bit like this:

She said, "Your talk today at our district meeting was inspiring."

I replied, "So was your lesson on helping people to commit."

She then said, "You are quite a missionary."

I answered, "Thank you. So are you."

She asked, "How do you feel about your mission so far?"

"I love it with all my heart. I didn't know when I came that I would feel so strongly about the gospel and all that it means."

"I can tell," she replied. She then added, "The people here love you."

"They love you too." I said.

Then I looked at her. She was looking ahead, and not at me. She looked so radiant, almost glorious. I had never really seen her before. I mean, I had never seen her soul.

I thought to myself, "When I get home, I hope I can find someone like her."

The bridge came down and we crossed and joined our companions. Soon the Sisters turned off to go to their home and we went on down the road to ours.

A few weeks later Sister Burnham finished her mission and departed for home. I often thought of her during the last few months of my mission. I admired her so deeply. I recalled the way that I felt when she was near. Thinking of her made me happy. During those last days of my mission, I had many dreams of what I would like to accomplish in my future life. It occurred to me that my dreams could come true if I was with her. I then realized that little by little, I had not fallen in love with Sister Burnham. I had fallen in love with all the many things that she was.

That story, of falling in love with Sister Burnham, is like unto the foundation of what I desire to say in this book. In a sense, a priesthood man needs to fall in love with the Gospel of Jesus Christ and with His Church the way that I fell in love with Sister Burnham. I met her, I learned a bit about her and then I learned more. As time passed I learned much more. I admired her. I wanted to be the way she was and then I loved her.

## FALLING IN LOVE WITH THE CHURCH, THE GOSPEL, AND THE LORD

So it was with the Church, the Gospel, and the Lord. As a young person I met the Church. As time passed, I learned a bit more about the Church. I learned the doctrines of Christ. I learned of His example and I wanted to be like Him. I learned of His love, I came to have faith in Him and I wanted to change and be like Him. I wanted to take upon myself His name. I wanted to have the Holy Ghost to teach me. Gradually, I learned more, and I admired the truths of the Gospel that were taught in the scriptures and in the Church. I wanted to be the way the Church taught me to be. Gradually I began to fall in love with the Church and all that it taught, and all that it did for my life and for my soul.

## THE HISTORY OF MY LOVE FOR THE CHURCH

My own romance with the Church began with the things that I did as a boy, then during my teenage years and finally into middle and older age. Your romance with the Church may not have begun as a boy for one reason or another. You may now be a man who desires to fall in love with the Church. I want to tell you in more detail, how I fell in love with the Church.

Many years ago the closing bell of the Harrington Elementary School rang at three-thirty on a Tuesday afternoon. It was time to begin my journey to Primary. I'd leave through the north door of the school and walk past the Apollo Dance Hall. From there I would continue east for two blocks until I came to the old creek bed. I'd walk along the east bank of this creek in a diagonal direction for three blocks. Then off to the east I could see the Fourth Ward meeting house. I liked to get there a few minutes early so that I would have time to play on the grass, or on the snow, along with the other dozen or so boys. We would play "pomp, pomp pull away," or "red rover red rover send George right over." We would play until Laura Timpson and the other leaders called us inside for Primary. I loved Primary. I loved Primary so much that for five straight years I never missed a single time of attending. I don't recall much of what I learned in Primary. I just remember that I loved it, and I loved my teachers and leaders. I loved my green Bandello and the little cloth emblems that I received by doing small acts of goodness. My mom sewed each of these emblems onto my Bandello. With pride, I wore this Bandello around my neck. I loved singing the song, "I Am a Boy Trail Builder." I felt that I was truly a boy trail builder.

During the last year of my Primary career, my teacher, Laura Timpson, helped me prepare a talk to give in Sacrament Meeting. The subject she and I selected was, a good spring would flow with good water, and a bad spring would flow with bad water. I gave the talk. I shall never forget the feelings that I had as I stood up front giving that short sermon. I could feel every word that I was saying, I could feel the power of the Holy Ghost. It was the happiest feelings I had ever known.

When I was twelve years old I became a deacon. I loved being a deacon. Mom used the Montgomery Ward's catalog to order me a navy blue suit, my first suit. I could tell by the way she looked at me when I put that suit on that I looked good in navy blue.

I loved passing the sacrament. I was good at knowing how to hold the tray, and I knew how to stand straight and tall. When the priests handed me the shining silver sacrament tray, I knew just where to go.

When I became a teacher in the Aaronic Priesthood, I loved to prepare the sacrament. Herbie Palowski and I tried to never get a drop of water on the silver tray.

Then, as a priest, I was able to say the sacred sacramental prayers. I loved doing that. I loved helping people receive the sacrament.

## WHEN LOVE WANES

At that stage in my youth, I didn't know all that I wanted to do in my life; however I was falling deeply in love with the Church. Then, with the stresses of growing, I was on occasion, a bit unfaithful to the Church. Whenever this happened, I felt I was betraying the Church and that made me uncomfortable. Not bad things just drifting a bit away. During those difficult years, the powers pulling me away were a bit more powerful than the ones keeping me close to the Church. My love for the Church cooled; however, the feelings pleading with me to be faithful were still there.

I recall on a warm, Sunday afternoon, I was playing croquet on the front lawn with my older brother and his friends. In the midst of a critical moment in the game, my mother came out on the porch and called out to me, "George it is time to come in and get ready for church."

I shouted back, "I'm not going tonight."

She turned and went back inside, and I continued to play.

A few minutes later I tried not to look as she passed us to go out the gate and down the road to the church house. However, even without looking, I sensed that she was looking at me and holding back the tears. After the game ended, we all got in Elmo Murdock's Model A Ford to go riding around town. As we went down Main Street, I hoped some of the kids from school would see me riding around with the older guys so they would think I was important.

Then, almost by fate, we passed the Fourth Ward church house just after the meeting ended. My mother was coming down the stairs holding onto the rail so she wouldn't fall. Usually I was there to help her down the stairs. We just kept on driving, and my mother walked home alone. Usually I was there to walk home with her.

As I rode the last few blocks to our house I kept thinking about my mother sitting alone in the meeting, then walking down the steep stairs without anyone there to hold her arm and help her. Then, thinking about her walking home alone caused all the fun I was trying to have to fly out the Model A window. When I arrived home, Mother was there in the kitchen doing some dishes. I went to her side and said softly, "Sorry, Ma. I just want you to know you will never have to go to church alone again as long as I'm alive."

My dedication to the Church faded a bit at times, but the Church was always on my mind. Breaking up with the Church was indeed hard for me to do. So I hung on.

## Falling Back In Love With All My Heart

Falling back in love with the Church happened in a multitude of ways. First I became an elder. A few days before I became an elder I was asked to visit with the stake president. I remember the interview:

"Do you know the Church is true?" The President asked.

"Yes I do," I replied.

"Do you obey the Word of Wisdom?"

"I do," I answered.

"What about your relationship with girls?"

"No problem. Most of them just ignore me."

"Do you know why I'm asking you these questions?"

"No."

"We would like you to become an elder. Would you like that?"

"I would really like that."

"All right, next Sunday it will happen."

That night at my bedside I told the Lord, "If you let me be an elder, I promise you I will never swear or tell any bad jokes, or do anything wrong with girls." I told Him many more things, but He never answered me. The next Sunday I became Elder George D. Durrant and I have been different ever since.

I just said that He never answered me. What I mean is that He didn't give me any special feeling at that time. However, His answer to my prayer has continued on ever since that wonderful night when I renewed my love with Him and His glorious Gospel.

## MY LOVE FOR THESE SACRED THINGS GREW

As a new elder, I went home teaching with my former seminary teacher Raymond Bailey. We visited an older widow. I had decided that if I was going to be a good home teacher I needed to be able to discuss the weather, so I spoke right up and said something about how cold it was outside. I talked about politics a little and how I loved Roosevelt and was not sure Truman was as good a man as Roosevelt was. I even taught a little of the discussion. I felt really good about my new role as a home teacher. I gave the prayer. Then she said something that really set me back. She asked us to give her a blessing. I did not know how to do that and I became a bit frightened. Fortunately we did not have any consecrated oil. I was glad that we could not proceed with the blessing. But Brother Bailey said that we could go and get some.

As we rode along I told him, "Brother Bailey, I can't do this."

"Why?" he asked. "Aren't you worthy?"

"I'm worthy, but I don't know how." He then told me how to anoint her head and what to say. We gave her the blessing. When we finished she turned to me and took my hand into hers and caressed it. She looked up at me as tears streamed down her face.

She said, "I'm so glad that you are the kind of man who can come here and help give me a blessing."

I was so choked up with joy that I couldn't speak. I turned away and went out the door and stood alone on the porch to wait for Brother Bailey. I looked up at the stars and told Heavenly Father that was what I wanted to do with my life. I just wanted to go around giving people blessings. I loved the Lord so deeply that sacred night.

Then I was called on a mission. For two years I was courting the Lord. Just like a young lover courting his bride to be. He and I became closer and closer. I have not enough room in this book to tell of how my love grew for Him and the gospel during those two years.

So that is a brief history of how I fell in love with the Church.

## MORE IN LOVE NOW THAN EVER BEFORE

The other day in a temple sealing session I was with a group of eight patrons. One of the young sisters there told me that she was a great, great granddaughter of Hyrum Smith, the Prophet's brother. Another said she was the same relation to President John Taylor. My heart was already tender, because those, for whom we were serving as proxies, seemed so close by. When I thought of those early Church leaders such as Hyrum Smith and John Taylor, tears came to my eyes. I told those with me of my love for them and for the great heritage we shared. My heart was overflowing with love for our Heavenly Father and His Son Jesus Christ, for the prophets, and for all who did their part in making such sweet things as ordinances for the living and the dead. I have never felt a deeper love, or a purer joy.

## LOVE MOTIVATES YOU TO BE THE PRIESTHOOD LEADER OF YOUR FAMILY

The love I felt on that occasion in the temple and on so many other occasions motivate me to do gospel centered things because I "want to" and not because I "have to". What I am saying was illustrated by a senior missionary I once knew:

At a couples conference in the Kentucky Louisville Mission, ten senior couples sat in a circle in the front room of the mission home. Each husband was asked to take a minute to tell why he loved his wife. The answers were all heart warming and created a tender and loving atmosphere. Finally all others had spoken and it was time for the last husband to speak. This 75 year old backwoods man from Ohio clutched the hand of his grey haired wife, and said with deep emotion, "I love my wife because I just cain't help it." I'll never forget those words, "I love my wife because I just cain't help it." This good man's heart was so full of deep emotion for his wife that he just could not stop loving her.

You can feel such deep love for the Lord that you just can't help doing His will. You just can't help having integrity in your life, and in blessing the lives of your wife and children. You just can't help being as good or better in your private and in your family life as you are when you are in public. None of us can do from the outside in all the good things that we want by using our sheer willpower. We have to do it from the inside out. We have to have the Lord helping us. We have to do it together with Him. We have to do it out of the abundance of love in our heart. We have to do it because we just can't help it.

Out of this love, we will be able to do and be all that we need to do and be. Of course we will still falter, and become discouraged and tired. But even then we will know that the Lord approves of the path that we are on and the effort we are making. We will have the greatest feeling of all. We will have hope. We will know that in our family's journey, "All is well." We will have the inner strength to become a priesthood leader in our home and to become a Fine Old High Priest.

# PART II

---

# TEMPLE ORDINANCES AND COVENANTS BECOME THE FOUNDATION OF YOUR PRIESTHOOD LEADERSHIP

# CHAPTER 6
## ADMINISTERING AND RECEIVING YOUR SACRED ORDINANCES

I'm now a sealer at the Mount Timpanogos Temple. It is every bit as exciting to be a sealer as it was to be a deacon, teacher or a priest. The thrill of helping people make and keep sacred covenants with the Lord never diminishes. When I was set apart as a sealer by a member of the First Presidency, I was just as nervous as I had been when my Bishop ordained me a deacon.

### IN THE BEGINNING

The first sealings I performed were for the deceased. I tried to be calm, but my trembling hands showed the apprehension that I felt in my heart. I had tried to memorize the prayers, but I often faltered in the words I was speaking. Soon I was feeling something that I had never felt before. The veil between the people who were there to serve as proxies for the deceased and the deceased themselves seemed so thin. It seemed as though the spirits for whom we were doing the ordinances were there with us. I did not see any of them; however I could sense that they were there.

As the session ended I felt a great love for the people who had come to do these vicarious sealings. These good people were acting for those who never had the opportunity to receive these ordinances for themselves. As they departed from the room we had a difficult time saying goodbye. We were all united in the feelings of love. We knew that together we had just done something that goes beyond the word "important." It was much like the feelings that I had had as a deacon and as a priest when

I had been part of the administration of the sacrament. I'm glad someone wrote the hymn, "Sweet is the Work," for it is only in those words that I can express the feelings of how it feels to do the sacred work of the Lord.

## PERFORMING THE FIRST MARRIAGE

One week later, I performed my first marriage for a living couple. As I sat outside the sealing room waiting for the couple to arrive, I felt my old fears returning. I shouldn't say fears, for it was not that, it was just a feeling that what I was about to do was so important that I wasn't sure that I could do it in the sacred manner in which it should be done. I met the couple and sensed they were filled with hope. They were glad to be there in the holy temple with the one they loved with all their heart. I entered the room and said, "This is the first wedding I have ever performed in the temple." I added, "I wish my wife was here to tell me where to stand." They laughed and I felt a bit more comfortable.

I immediately felt the sacredness of what was happening and somehow thoughts came. Before I began, I had not known what to say, but the Lord filled the room, with His Spirit, and all was well.

After the ceremony the bride and groom expressed their gratitude and love to me for what I had done. After they had departed I was alone in the room, and for a few brief seconds I lingered there. I knew with all my heart that the wonderful couple could be together forever. The love and gratitude I felt caused me to look up and thank the Lord for something as beautiful as a temple marriage.

Over the years I have become more confident in officiating at sealing ceremonies. Though my anxieties have lessened, I still dream of doing as well now as I did on that first occasion when I knew what was about to happen was not up to me, it was all up to the Lord.

## A More Detailed Account Of A Temple Marriage

Now I will describe my feelings as a temple sealer at a temple marriage. I will merge the facts and feeling of several weddings so that I will not be describing one specific wedding, and of course I will not discuss the wording of the ceremony, nor will I describe any of the sacred temple ordinances or covenants.

## A Temple Marriage Through The Eyes Of A Sealer

It is the morning of a cold, wintry day. Three inches of snow fell last night. I, the appointed sealer, arrive at the temple an hour before the wedding is to begin. As I walk along in my big overcoat, I imagine the bride is a bit upset because she knows it will be cold after the wedding as they go outside for pictures. This and other concerns will cause her to have much on her mind in addition to the wedding.

I know the groom better than I know her. I have heard that he was a great missionary in a far away place, and he hopes to become an engineer. He was a fine high school athlete and is on his college baseball team.

By the time I go up the stairs to the area of the temple where sealings are performed, it is just forty minutes until time to begin. I feel tinges of anxiety as I take care of the required paper work. Soon the two witnesses are seated at my side at a small table where they will sign the license and the wedding certificate.

I learn that one of the witnesses is the groom's brother. He informs me that his father will not be at the wedding. I feel some regret about that. I ask the bride's father to tell me the very best thing about her. I sense I have touched a tender nerve as he pauses and then says, "Ever since she was a little girl she has wanted to do the right thing. She came to the temple for the first time last week and she loved it. She loves the underdog. For her whole life she has been a pure joy to me and her mother."

I then turn and ask the groom's brother to tell me about him. He quietly replies, "He is real excited about this. He is a great man." After the witnesses sign the papers I advise them of their important role, and then invite them to go to room six where the wedding will begin in ten minutes.

I then walk down the hall to a chair just outside the sealing room where the wedding will take place. Sitting there I strive to prepare myself for the sacred event which I will be part of. I silently pray for three things: first, that my heart will be filled with love, second that my sins will be forgiven, and third that the veil between heaven and earth will be very thin. I know that if those three things happen, what I will do in leading this grand ordinance will be in accord with all the Lord would desire.

Soon the guide comes down the hall with the bride and groom. I stand and greet them, and tell them how grateful and honored I am to be part of this glorious event.

After the bride and groom are seated in the room, I enter. I shake hands with the two mothers who are seated by their son and daughter. I then take my place standing at the head of the alter. I ask if there are any grandparents of either the bride or groom in the room. Younger people start pointing them out to me. I feel a great love for these older folks who have had so much to do with all that the bride and groom believe and are.

I ask if there are any bishops or stake presidents there. A young bishop raises his hand. I know he has a major investment in this couple. His wife holds his hand tightly. I am thrilled when someone whispers, "His mission president and his wife are here." I turn to look at them. I ask, "Was he a good missionary?" They both say in unison, "He was the best." I see three young men on the back row. I suppose that they are the groom's friends. I see some young ladies and feel that they must be the bride's college roommates. The room has seats for sixty people and it is nearly full. There is a sense of oneness in the room. All who are there love the bride and groom. All of them love the Lord.

I know the couple is not there to hear a long talk. They are there to get married. So I know there is not time for many words. In ten minutes or so I often say something like this:

*"When you came in the room you were filled with love and hope and faith. However, you were still single; each on your*

*own path of life. Now in just a few more minutes that will all change and your two paths will merge into one. From then on and forever the two of you will be on the same path because the Lord's holy seal will be upon the ordinance of your marriage. Thus your journey will be together all through this life, then into the spirit world and to the resurrection and then into the Millennium and on into the Celestial Kingdom."*

As I speak words such as these, I feel the Spirit of the Lord more strongly than I feel it in any other setting. I know that the couple and all of us in the room are right in the center of the Lord's plan of happiness, and that what we are doing is the Lord's way and indeed the marriage will be for time and all eternity. I speak for another several minutes about the ordinances and covenants and promises of the endowment which they have each received previously. I realize as I speak that the couple have much on their minds and are not as able to relax and listen as are the other people in the room. I know that the bride and groom don't need to fully understand the words as much as they need to feel the Spirit of the Lord. I discern that they feel the words.

I wish I could give a full account of the words I say to the couple, but any more would be too much. All sealers have a little different approach in these preliminary teachings. But each of them talk about the blessings of the temple, and each has the Spirit of the Lord, and each has the sealing power to bind on earth and it will be bound in heaven.

Then the couple is directed to their places at the alter. The room is totally silent except for a few sniffles among some of those who sense the profound importance of what is about to happen. I cannot express how sacred it is to act as the voice of the Lord in the words that are said as the couple accepts each other as their eternal husband or wife, and as they agree to forever keep this new covenant of marriage and all the other covenants they have made.

Then the most important of all words will be spoken. Words backed up by the authority of the Lord, words which unite the couple in marriage for time and for all eternity. When the final amen is said, the couple leave the alter and stand together as husband and wife forever. They look into the mirrors as a reminder of the eternal nature of their marriage.

During the last few minutes in the sealing room the parents, the grandparents and then the others pass by the couple and quietly wish them well. The grandfathers often take the most time with the couple. They, feeling the Spirit of the Lord, have so much they would like to tell the new bride and groom. Finally all are gone from the room except the newlyweds, the parents and me. All hearts are filled with joy. It is the most tender of all moments.

The bride is no longer worried about pictures out in the cold. She knows because of what she has just felt that all that matters most about her wedding day is now complete. Now pictures, dinners and receptions seem far less important. The bride and groom want to linger in the room for it is here that they have felt the sweetest feelings that can ever be felt. I invite them to come back in fifty years and say to each other, "This is where it all began."

Finally the couple leaves the room, no longer on two paths, but together on one path forever. As they depart, I long for them to stay on the path the Lord has set; the path that will give them happiness in this life and eternal life forever. As I close the room and make my way along the hall to the office I say to myself, "It is good to be a sealer."

# CHAPTER 7
## YOUR FIRST TIME AT THE TEMPLE

It was a landmark day in your eternal destiny when you came to the temple to be endowed. In all likelihood you remember that day well. I know I vividly remember the day I was endowed.

### MY FIRST TIME AT THE TEMPLE

The year was 1953. I was in the mission home in Salt Lake City preparing to leave for my mission to England. In the afternoon meeting the mission president reminded us that the next morning we would go to the temple to be endowed. I panicked, for I realized I had forgotten to bring my temple recommend as I had been told to do in an official letter.

While the other missionaries went to dinner, I hurried to a nearby phone booth to call my bishop to tell him of my desperate problem. I knew he worked for the highway patrol. I opened the phone directory to find the number for that agency, but to my distress, there were at least twenty phone listings for the highway patrol. I ran my finger down the list and called a number.

A lady answered, "Highway patrol."

I blurted out, "I need to talk to Mel Grant."

She replied, "How did you know he was here? He seldom comes to this office, but he is standing here talking to me right now."

Bishop Grant took the phone and I explained my situation. He felt bad because he believed that he was to blame. He said, "I'm in Salt Lake now, but I can drive fast. I will go to American Fork. I will sign your recommend and I will get the stake president to sign it. We know you are worthy because we just interviewed you for your mission. Then I will give the recommend to Patrolman Evans. He can also drive fast. He will bring it to you tonight."

That night, as I sat in a meeting with the other two hundred missionaries, a highway patrolman entered the rear door and came to the front and whispered to the president. The president came to the microphone and announced, "This officer would like to speak to Elder George Durrant." All eyes were on me as I followed the officer from the room. Out in the hall he gave me a "ticket" to enter the temple.

The next morning I went to the temple to be endowed and going there has made all the difference.

As I made my way out of the Salt Lake Temple that cold November morning in 1953, I didn't fully understand all I had just experienced. I did know that somehow I was different than when I had come in, but I didn't understand why. I knew that I had covenanted with the Lord, but I didn't know specifically what it was I had agreed to do. I knew I had been promised blessings, but I didn't quite know what those blessings were. Now, many years later, I do know what happened on that day and that makes me glad.

## LOOKING BACK MAKES THINGS CLEAR

Through the years I have found that it is in looking back on what happened to me in the temple on that day long ago which has enriched my life. To illustrate the value of looking back to our covenants let me go back in time...

## LOOKING BACK ON MY BAPTISM

I was baptized and received the Holy Ghost at age eight in the old Tabernacle in downtown American Fork. However the truth is, for the next 10 years I did not think much about what my baptismal covenant meant. I'm sure that during those critical years from boyhood to young manhood the Holy Ghost helped me on many occasions. But I never really consciously paid much attention to what the Holy Ghost meant to me. Though not a bad boy, I was far from firm in the faith. I never really knew just exactly where I stood on matters related to my eternal destiny. I, as someone said of someone else, 'had both feet firmly planted in mid air'. I spent a lot of time gazing at the large and spacious building that Lehi saw in his dream the large attractive building without a foundation.

In a ninth grade class I sat behind a girl I adored. Each Friday we were assigned to give a short talk. Every Friday when the teacher called the role each of us could answer "prepared" or "unprepared." I feared giving a talk, so for weeks I answered, "Unprepared."

One day when I said, "unprepared," the girl in front of me turned and looked at me and asked, "Why don't you get prepared?" I decided that I would get prepared.

The next week when my name was called I answered, "Prepared." The girl turned back to me and smiled. When it was my turn to speak, I fearfully walked to the front, faced the class and began to speak. I stood firmly with my feet planted on the solid floor. Suddenly I felt secure and good; it was a fine talk. I returned to my seat and the girl smiled. I sat down and thought, "From now on I will always be prepared." But I wasn't. Sometimes I was prepared and sometimes I wasn't. I was not dependable. I alternated between being wishy-washy and washy-wishy. I never knew what I would be; I never knew where I stood.

When I was in high school I agreed to sing with three other guys in an assembly. Just before the student assembly I chickened out. The girl in charge of the assembly was really angry at me and I felt bad. I tell you these things to make the point that I did well sometimes and sometimes I didn't. I don't ever recall thinking, "I'm baptized, and I ought to be good and dependable." Looking back I wish I would have done better in those days, but alas that was long ago.

## Finally On My Mission I Knew

At 19, I was called on a mission to England. I was there to help people become baptized, and to be forgiven of their sins. That made me think back on my own baptism and I wondered about my own sins. I was glad that through my faith in Jesus Christ and my repentance and my baptism I was forgiven. Finally I loved looking back on my baptism. I wished as I was baptizing others that I could meet the man who baptized me. I wanted to thank him because, though I had never seen him since my baptism, I loved him. I loved the sacrament because I could remember my baptismal covenants. Oh sure, there were still days when I took things for granted, when I did not think as seriously and gratefully as I should have. But in a large measure I had changed just as I promised I would when I was baptized many years before. I knew then, that looking back on the covenants we have made, is vital to our spiritual well being.

## The Need For Constant Recommitment

As a missionary I was at a meeting with a family who was investigating the gospel. Their uncle, who was a professor of philosophy at the local university, came unexpectedly to the meeting. I was teaching about Joseph Smith and his First Vision. I was nervous about what the bearded philosopher thought of my teachings so I began to water down the message. Instead of teaching the vision as a fact, I said, "We believe Joseph Smith saw God." I quickly added, "Of course you may not believe that. That is all right because I know it is a story that is hard to believe." I became wishy-washy in all that I said. Again, it was as if I had both feet planted in mid air.

As we rode our bikes home, I was very discouraged. Why was I so indecisive? Later that night I apologized to my companion about what I had done, and I promised him and myself that from then on I would be true to my faith, and I usually was. I made the same promise to the Lord in my evening prayer. In the months that followed there were still times when I was weak and seemed to have no foundation. My greatest disappointments have always come when I have known where I should stand and instead of standing there I have stood on lower ground.

## THINKING BACK ON MY TEMPLE COVENANTS

Before my mission I went to the temple just one time. After being a missionary for a year or so I could recall very little about what I had experienced in the temple. As missionaries we didn't say much about the temple in our discussions with investigators because there was not yet a temple in England. The temple covenants had blurred in my memory. I was not sure what I had covenanted to do in the temple. I was a good missionary not perfect, but a good missionary. It was not until I came home from my mission and a month later got married, that the temple began to take its rightful place as the foundation of my life.

## ALWAYS REMEMBERING

So what does all this mean to me? It means that it is wonderful to prepare and make covenants, but the life-changing part of covenants is in remembering them. Making covenants is the *promise* to be a fine old high priest, but remembering and keeping those covenants is the way to *become* a fine old high priest. Think back on the temple and the endowment you received there. Consider again the covenants and promises you made. Recall all the amazing blessings that were pronounced upon you. Think again of the principles you learned. These sacred truths will serve as the foundation for your priesthood leadership in the family.

You may say, "I can't really remember that much about the temple." My answer to that is, the best way to remember all that took place in your endowment is to go back to the temple and have an experience there for someone else. You will help the deceased receive eternal blessings but you will also remember again your own temple covenants and blessings.

## Go To The Temple Often

You should go to the temple often enough that you can recall in detail all you were taught, the covenants you made there and the promises that were made to you. Thinking back you will recall many sacred experiences. Remember the first ordinances; you were given specific blessings of body and spirit that would help you understand and live the gospel of Jesus Christ. You were also blessed to more fully be part of the sacred Atonement of Jesus Christ. I know of your deep love for the Savior and for all that He has done for you. You were promised that you had a grand, eternal destiny. To help you follow that path to that destiny, you were given the blessing of wearing a "garment." The garment that you now wear serves as a constant reminder to stay on the path that will lead you to your promised exaltation.

As you go back to the temple to help another, you will remember all that happened to you when you received your endowment. You will recall again the creation of the earth and our opportunities in mortality. You will remember the role of the Savior and the priesthood and you will remember the covenants that you made. If these things are not clear in your mind, return to the temple often enough that they will be clear.

## Remembering Again

I was only able to attend the temple once before my mission. When I came home in December I was in love with Marilyn and we were married in January in the Salt Lake Temple. I don't believe anyone had ever been as in love as I was with Marilyn. I was so glad she had agreed to marry me.

Much to my regret, I had not returned to the temple in the month between my mission and my marriage so the details of my endowment were not clear. For that reason we decided to have our marriage at noon so we could attend the temple that morning and act as proxies for others so we could refresh our knowledge of our covenants.

It was good to be in the Creation Room in the Salt Lake Temple not only as a patron, but also as an artist. I could recall sitting there two years earlier and being in awe of the beautiful murals that covered the walls and ceiling of that room. Two years later, I felt that way again only more so. As I sat there I had a flood of memories come back into my mind and heart, and during the next two hours I learned and covenanted anew. It was so good to be back in the Holy Temple and to have the temple back in me. I was on my way to becoming the priesthood leader in my family and I was happy.

# CHAPTER 8
## TEMPLE MARRIAGE WAS THE BEGINNING OF YOUR FAMILY PATH

Among my short list of favorite movies is "The Wizard of Oz". I first saw this amazing movie at the Cameo Theater in American Fork when I was a young boy. I loved Dorothy, the Tin Man, the Scarecrow and the Lion. I was frightened by the wicked witch and her army of flying monkeys. I was totally fascinated by the *Yellow Brick Road.* I wanted to arise from my seat, go to the front of the theater and jump into the silver screen so I could journey down the yellow brick road with Dorothy and the others. It was called the *Yellow Brick Road,* but to me it seemed more like a path. I have always loved paths.

Thinking about going down a path into the unknown woods is a pleasant and exciting thought. I suppose that is why I like to think of life as a journey down a winding and challenging path into the woods.

As youngsters, we travel with our family down the path of life. We make a few individual side trips, but generally we are on the path with our family. As we mature into young adults our side trips become more frequent until we are on our own individual path.

## TWO PATHS BECOME ONE

Before your marriage, your wife was on her individual path to her eternal destiny, and you were on yours. Then a great and marvelous change occurred. The two of you met, fell in love and came to the temple. When you walked into the sealing room you were each filled with hope and faith and love but you were still single. Then you each came to the alter and something wonderful happened. During that holy ceremony of marriage, the Lord's seal was placed on the ordinance, making your union valid not only for time but for all eternity.

When you departed from the sealing room you were no longer single. You were married. As you walked out of the sealing room you were no longer on two paths. Instead the two of you were on the same path. Your two paths were merged into one eternal journey. This path will lead the two of you through this earth life, through the spirit world, to the resurrection, through the millennium and on to the Celestial Kingdom.

Dorothy and her friends in their fictitious journey were headed for Oz. You and your wife are headed for the royal courts on high where you will, as was promised in the temple, be exalted with glory.

No matter how good the path you were on as an individual, it is not nearly as fulfilling and joyous as is the merged path you and your wife entered into at the time of your marriage.

## OF COURSE THERE WILL BE PROBLEMS

One of the major reasons for your happiness is that the two of you will have your share of problems. Soon the two of you shall, as did Dorothy and her friends, enter the land of lions and tigers and bears. It will be as if you suddenly see a sign that says, "Turn back while there is still time."

## SO IT WAS FOR MARILYN AND ME

For Marilyn and me the first lion that appeared in our path was that we did not have any money, nor did we have an apartment to live in. We could live with our parents but that was not our path. We wanted our own path. We prayed and went to the BYU housing office. There was a little apartment that was too small for others because it was a combination kitchen, bedroom and living room all in one. Because it was only big enough for Munchkins, it was half the price of the other apartments that were listed. The price was just right for our meager funds; even so it took nearly all of our money.

Our plan was that I would continue in school and Marilyn would go to work, but she had no job. We prayed and she went to the phone company in Provo. She had worked at the same company in Salt Lake City. They said they had no job but while she was there the phone rang. It was an employee calling to say she wanted to stay home with her baby and needed to quit her job. The man gave Marilyn the job on the spot.

And so it went. Each time we saw a lion, a tiger, or bear or a sign that said turn back, we marched right through and moved closer to our divine destiny. With each of those challenges we became more like our Heavenly Father wanted us to be. We had many other problems because the Lord loved us.

## YOUR DESTINY

If I were speaking to you and your wife about your temple marriage, this is what I would say to you:

This earth was created so that the two of you could be born here, grow up here, meet here, fall in love here, get married here, have children here, and raise your children in the Lord here. Not only has Heavenly Father given you this place and this opportunity, but He has also given you a "plan of happiness" to help guide you along your path to your eternal destiny.

As you received your sacred endowment, you were taught of God's grand plan for your success and joy. You were shown that the earth was created so that you could come here and have the opportunity to grow by following Jesus Christ. At the heart of this plan a Savior would be provided to make it possible for you to return to our Heavenly Father and to gain immortality and eternal life.

The two of you were taught in the temple about the great role Adam and Eve played in your eternal destiny. They had it comfortable and easy in the Garden of Eden, but they chose to go out into the world where they could live by faith and follow the plan of happiness; not by force, but in accordance to their own agency. Adam and Eve found the world outside the garden to be a very difficult place. In that unkind world they had some heartbreaking experiences within their family. It seems as though heartbreaking experiences are almost always in the family. That is because the family can handle it, and in time can turn heartbreak into joy. The two of you, just as did Adam and Eve, will have problems as you go along the path of life.

It is exciting to have problems. It would be no fun to play baseball if the other team did not show up for the game. In life the other team always shows up. The other team plays pretty hard. They win a few innings, but you win the game. In meeting this strong opposition you become quite the players. You become more like Heavenly Father and Jesus Christ, more compassionate, more understanding, and more faithful in keeping your covenants. As a matter of fact, the only way the two of you can get to where you desire to go is through the middle of the oppositions that will often be right in your pathway.

## Our Greatest Heartbreak

The greatest heartbreak I ever faced was when I finished basic training in the Army and received orders to go to Korea. Marilyn was to deliver our first child soon and I could not bear the thought of leaving her and our child to go to the other side of the world. We prayed that something would come up so that we would not have to be apart. I called the General at my camp and he patiently listened and said, "I know how you feel Private Durrant, but what kind of an Army would it be if we could not send married men to where we need them." He was kind and fortunately I did not get in trouble for calling him. I wrote to my Senator and he said he understood, but could do nothing.

As time drew near for our separation we prayed with all our hearts for a miracle. Marilyn literally soaked her pillow with tears. The time was near for me to go. We still hoped for a miracle but no miracle came. We could not bear to say goodbye.

We prayed for strength and our prayers were answered. I still had to go, but we received strength and that strength lasted all through the long months we were apart.

## THE PRAYER FOR STRENGTH IS ALWAYS ANSWERED

When Adam sensed the problems that he faced in the world, he turned to the Lord in prayer. He wanted to know that the Lord would hear his prayer. The two of you know that all prayers get heard even though they are not always answered in the desired way. The only prayer that is always answered is the prayer for strength. As you pray for strength, you receive the strength of the Lord, and you will make it through any and all opposition that confronts you. That is what Adam and Eve did and they made it, and so will you. In facing your problems and heartaches with the strength of the Lord, the two of you will become more like the Lord stronger, more compassionate and more understanding.

## HELPING OTHERS THROUGH THEIR STORMS

Lest you think I speak too much of problems, I quickly add that most of the time the two of you will sail on calm seas. There will be times of storms and rough waters and if you are not having a storm in your life, someone you know and love will be having a storm in theirs. The two of you will help them through their storm you are good at that. People love and trust you. As you help others through their storm you will become more like our Savior more sensitive and caring. Thus you will be ever closer to your goal of exaltation.

## YOUR OFFICIAL ASSIGNMENT TO BE THE PRIESTHOOD LEADER IN YOUR HOME

On that holy day when you were married, you became the priesthood leader in your family. Your wife, in a great act of faith, gave herself to you. She knew she would be secure and loved in your gentle and mighty priesthood hands. As you live and lead in righteousness, when your wife speaks of you to others she will gladly say, "It seems that my husband's greatest desire is obey the Lord." No woman minds following a man who follows the Lord, because he is a kind and loving man whose overriding and constant desire is to help his family.

You and your wife will go down the path together as equal partners, but you will make certain that you use proper priesthood leadership that will lead your family to make and keep sacred gospel covenants. You, as the husband and father, will stand firmly on your temple foundation and will lead out in tenderly teaching those principles which will help you and your family to stay on the path. The path will lead you all to your family's eternal destiny. I remind you again, that as you go down the path of life, you and your wife will walk side by side, always looking ahead, saying and praying together, "What now? Where now? How now?" You will be equal partners forever in obeying the covenants you have made in the temple.

## THE CHILDREN WILL COME

We love Adam and Eve for all they did for us, and for all they taught us. They also made choices that made it possible for them, and for us, to have children. The two of you will have wonderful children. I speak for your children because can you imagine what a blessing it is to born to a mother like your wife, and to a father like you. So I give you this reminder, "Do not stop having children until you have had your last one." Parents do not know what they would have done without their last one, or their first one, or all the middle ones. The only way to know the joy that comes from having children in your family is to have the blessing of becoming a father and a mother.

## YOU CAN DO THIS

I love paths that lead into the unknown. I love paths that lead through lions and tigers and bears. I love paths that have signs that say, "Turn back; there is danger and uncertainty along the path." Courage and strength are needed to make it through the tough places. Fathers need to fight off bears that come into the family's mind and heart. I love paths that require faith.

# CHAPTER 9
## LEADING YOUR FAMILY ALONG THE LORD'S PATH

Priesthood leadership is best illustrated by envisioning a family making their way along a narrow path leading back to our Heavenly Father. The leader of the family is the father, and at his side is the mother. The path often forks and decisions must be made as to which is the correct path. Fortunately, there are signs at each crossroad that will direct the family to remain on the right path.

### NEVER TURN BACK

I love to see a family walk along a path. I like to see a father who is willing to lead the way along that path; a father who holds his wife and children close, a father who is willing and able to lead his family to their eternal destiny, and a father who will never turn back in sunshine nor rain.

As a father leads his family along the long path there will be lions and tigers and bears all along the way. But turning back to find an easier path is not an option. I liken the following hiking experience to leading my family to the mountain top of our family destiny:

In the early 1980s I determined to climb Mt. Olympus, the nine-thousand-foot mountain that rises high above the Salt Lake Valley floor. My eleven-year-old son Mark and I arose at five o'clock in the morning to make the climb. It was still pitch black as we began to walk down the rough road that leads along the side of the mountain to the point where the trail begins.

We had not gone more than a hundred yards when I tripped over an unseen rock. Despite my efforts to keep from falling, I twisted my ankle and fell forward to the hard earth.

Mark, wondering what had happened, was greatly concerned. As I lay there on the ground, my ankle felt uncomfortably injured. With some effort I was able to stand up. I decided to try to walk. As I did so, I found that the pain seemed to subside.

The switchback trail led us higher and higher. I began to wish my ankle would hurt more so that I could have a legitimate reason to return home. But I could not disappoint my son so I kept going.

After much stopping, catching my breath, and forcing myself on, we came to a grove of pine trees that were a considerable distance up the mountain. The top of the mountain gradually seemed to be getting reachable.

We started up the rocks. Now it was a matter of pulling ourselves up large boulders. But just as I thought we had it made, the way became the most difficult of all. I pulled myself up one rock after another. We wound our way through chasms between giant boulders. It took us another half an hour to go only a short way, because I had to rest so often. Finally, completely out of energy, I was at the top of Mt. Olympus.

As this story shows, first comes a decision such as, "I will lead my family to our eternal goal." But then we encounter sprained ankles from tripping over little rocks of becoming lax in obedience to prayers, scripture reading and family home evening.

The journey gets more and more difficult as the world encroaches on family time. It is tempting to give up and turn back; to find a trail to a foothill instead of a mountain peak. Next comes fatigue because of the energy it takes to keep going day after day and year after year. And when we are nearly there we encounter giant boulders placed in our path by a world whose values are in turmoil.

But we do not turn back. Lions, tigers and bears move aside at our coming. And finally we reach the top and our joy is full. It has not always been easy but it has been worth it.

## BE NOT AFRAID

Your children need you to calm their fears even though you may have fears of your own.

I remember being on a camping trip with my family. We pitched our tent in a lonely place under some trees near a small stream. As we were going to sleep, we could all hear a noise just outside of our tent. The children asked if it was a bear. I told them that it was just a little chipmunk but in my heart I wondered if it was a bear. I was as frightened as they were but I knew I had to reassure them. And I did.

There will sometimes be scary noises in your wife and children's hearts. The sounds of the fears of feeling inadequate in sports, social life and other matters and circumstances. You will fear too, but you are to be the voice of reassurance. You are to be a calming influence. And who will reassure you? The Lord. He will give you courage because you are a priesthood man.

Our family once went to Yellowstone National Park. In those days the bears would come up to our car. We kept the windows up. That night we rented a little cabin in the woods. We were all a bit nervous. I asked my little five-year-old Kathryn to pray for us. She said, "Heavenly Father bless the doors and the windows and help them to stay closed real tight so that no bears can get in here tonight." We all felt safer after the prayer; including me.

Prayer can bring perfect love and perfect love drives out all fear. As you and your family go down the path of life, have a family prayer with every footstep. You, the priesthood leader of the family, must make sure this happens.

I felt like skipping prayer with Marilyn the other morning because I was in my office and she was in the other part of the house. But I knew better. So I left my writing and went to where Marilyn was. We talked for a few minutes about our plans for the day. Then she led us in prayer. I love to hear her pray. She prays in great detail. I repeat in my mind the words she speaks. It seems like I can almost see a special channel to heaven when she prays. We both say amen. I tell her of my love and I go back to my office. It is ten minutes later, but new ideas seem to be in a great rush to get from my mind onto paper.

## HAVE FUN ALONG THE WAY

Have fun along the path. The Mormon pioneers had fun as they were on the path across the plains, and you can too. Make your home such a fun place that your children will not want to run away. Instead they will want to run home. Fun experiences in the family are almost as important as spiritual experiences.

Our family had a tradition of eating scones on some wonderful evenings. One Sunday night I had a yearning for scones. I asked Marilyn, "Could you make some scones tonight if I help?"

She replied, "I'm so tired."

"I know," I said sympathetically. "I should not have asked."

She softened and replied, "If you would help, and see that things get cleaned up afterward, I guess I could do it."

I was overjoyed.

Soon the bread dough was cut into pieces about the size of a dollar bill. In a few minutes the first half dozen pieces of white dough had turned into light brown scones. Marilyn placed these delicious morsels in a large pan in the center of our round table. The other nine of us surrounded them with great glee, ready to pounce.

Before we began the feast I asked for silence and said, "Now it is time for our prayer. I will call upon our most outstanding family members to lead us in prayer." I looked at each family member while all waited for me to call on the chosen one.

Finally I said, "I will call on the best looking, the most popular and the most intelligent family member." I added, "I will call on the one that we all love and admire." By this time each of the eight children spoke up and said, "I gave the prayer last time."

Then after a pause, wherein I considered which one most needed to be honored, I called on him or her. The others groaned and moaned and complained, with good nature, that the one I had chosen did not fit the description I had given. The one chosen would look around with some degree of pride. All this was done in great humor and the children loved this ritual. I saw to it that each one had his or her turn at being the honored one.

Then after the prayer we would eagerly begin to eat. As we did so, Marilyn returned to the stove to cook more scones so that we could have them while they were hot. As we ate I would tell jokes and say many humorous things. At least I thought that they were humorous. I told one joke that I made up. I like to make up jokes. I asked, "What would you have if a man named Richard carved a boat out of a potato?" No one knew the answer. I replied with an all knowing tone, "You would have a Dick tater ship."

They all booed and told me that I had told a dumb joke. They always did that. I could tell wonderful jokes and they would not laugh. Marilyn would then tell a joke that was not nearly the quality of mine, and they would laugh long and loud. They did that to persecute me.

Before going on with the story I interject the fact that after dinner they would go to the phone and tell their friends the jokes I had told them. They would thus become popular with their friends because of the quality of these jokes.

Meanwhile back at the table.

As we began to eat, I would say, "Please pass the butter."

Marilyn would say. "It is margarine not butter."

I would reply, "I know that." But I would still call it butter because that made it taste better.

Marilyn would also fry eggs that were sunny side up. There is nothing more delicious than dipping a hot scone, dripping with butter, into an egg yoke and taking a big bite, and washing it down with a swallow of ice cold milk.

We would sit there and talk of all that was going on at school, and at church, and in the world of sports, and all sorts of serious and humorous matters. We would discuss, and laugh, and praise and eat, and laugh, and eat some more.

Then it was almost as if I could hear a knocking on the window. It was as if I opened the window, and blessings covered our whole family completely over.

—————————————————

No matter how far we have come there is still a long path ahead. So let's rise up and get going.

# CHAPTER 10
## THE TEMPLE IS THE FOUNDATION FOR YOUR FAMILY LEADERSHIP

---

Marilyn and I have lived in several apartments and eight houses. Two houses were constructed under our direction. We sometimes argued, as we picked out the exterior bricks, the windows, the colors for the walls, the floor coverings, and the type of wood for the cabinets. But, there was never a discussion with the contractor on whether we wanted the foundation to be made of wood, sand, or sawdust. It was just a given that the foundation would be made of unattractive, grey, hard cement.

First in the construction came the digging of the hole for the basement. Then the cement was poured into the trenches that had been dug for the footings, which were the connecting link between the earth and the house. Next came the foundation. The cement work seemed to take so long. We just wanted to get on to the important parts of the house: the walls, the windows and the roof. However our eagerness was tempered by the fact that we knew that we could never be safe in our new house without the foundation. For that stability and safety, we needed the grey, hard cement upon which to build the house.

## THE FOUNDATION OF PRIESTHOOD LEADERSHIP IN YOUR FAMILY

To be a priesthood leader in your family you must have a foundation. All the money, all the classes in psychology, all the marriage counseling, all the entertainment, all the schooling, all the vacations, all the sports, all the music, all the dance, all the success or acclaim can be the windows and the doors and the carpets and cabinets of our lives but they cannot be the foundation.

The "footings" of your life must be the Savior Jesus Christ. He must be your connection to truth and the eternities. Then, your endowment in the temple will be the foundation of your priesthood leadership in the home. Equal in importance to what you learned in the temple are the covenants that you made there. These covenants mark the path and lead the way to your eternal goal. When the two of you knelt at the alter in the Holy Temple to be married, as part of the words of the ceremony, you were invited to renew your promises to observe and keep all the covenants that you each made at your baptism and in receiving your endowment.

Recently I performed the marriage of my granddaughter in the Salt Lake Temple. Following the ceremony, I walked into the Celestial Room. I walked across to the sealing room that was just off the corner of the Celestial Room. I climbed the three stairs to the entrance of the room and looked inside. I had often wondered just which room it was where Marilyn and I were married more than fifty years earlier. I could not remember the details of the room; however I knew that this was the room.

The door was open and so I entered and stood near the alter. Then I slowly turned and looked at every detail of the room. I looked at the chairs. I could not recall, but I knew one of the chairs was where my mother had sat. In my mind I could see her. I could see the two chairs where my bishop and his wife had sat. In my mind I could see Marilyn and me kneeling at the alter.

I could hear again the words of Elder Kimball as he held his hands together interlocking his fingers. He said, "You and the Lord have locked your hands together through your covenants." He told us to keep our covenants. He pulled two fingers loose from the others and said, "If you do not obey a covenant you will pull apart from the Lord." Then he pulled two more fingers apart and said, "And if you don't obey another covenant more fingers will be pulled loose." Finally both his hands were apart and he told us that by not keeping our covenants we would separate ourselves from God and from all of our blessings.

After this recollection, I sat down. So much had happened since that day so long ago. I thought of each of our eight children and their spouses. I thought of the children and grandchildren who had come to bless our lives. I thought of our service in the Church. I remembered the wonderful opportunities we had had at home, in the Church and in our work. I thought of how my love for Marilyn was deeper now than it had ever been before. So many blessings had come to us because we held tight to our covenants. I knew that Marilyn and I had not been perfect. But I also knew we had been obedient and that made all the difference. I walked from "our" room and sat in the Celestial Room. My memory was now in full power.

I recalled many years ago when we had worked in the seminary program in Brigham City. I loved teaching the young people of that beautiful town. Part of my agreement when I was sent to Brigham City was that each day after the regular school day I would go to the seminary in which the Indian students attended. As time went by I came to love the Indian children, but I knew my future was with the other young people of the community.

Then, against all logic, I came to know that I should leave my work with the young people of Brigham City and go to the Reservation to do my work there among the Indians. When I announced my feelings to Marilyn, she was not impressed and told me that I was so good with the High School Seminary and they needed me as much or more than did the Indian children.

We had a lovely home in Brigham City. We were doing so well at the local seminary there. It was the perfect place to raise our children, but I could not get it out of my heart that we needed to go with the Indian part of the seminary program. That would mean we would need to move to a remote place on the Reservation. We did not want to go there. But we prayed and felt that we should give up our life in Brigham City and go into the "wilderness" to establish a new home.

We were obedient to the promptings and announced to the seminary officials that we desired a change. We wanted to work with the Indians. Those in charge of the seminary program told us that they had been praying that we would make that decision because we were much needed in that part of the work.

That decision opened unimaginable doors for us and flavored our entire lives from that time on.

I recalled when we were a young family; in 1965 the Church announced that all families should hold family home evenings each week. The First Presidency gave this prophetic utterance, "Families who have family home evenings are promised that love at home and obedience to parents will increase, and faith will develop in the hearts of the youth of Israel, and they will gain power to combat the evil influences and temptations that beset them."

At the time the family home evening program was introduced, we were hearing more and more about the widespread abuse of drugs. With deep gratitude I am grateful for family home evening because it became the heart and soul of our family life.

Recently I asked my grown children what they recall about our family home evenings. One wrote:

*Hey Dad,*

*My earliest memory of family home evening is when you included me in a story in the FHE manual that you wrote. It was about my friend Susan & me and our move from Provo to SLC when I was about 6. I felt very important to be included.*

*Some of my favorite home evenings were when we would each get $1 to spend in the grocery store. We would run around choosing stuff and not let the others know what we picked. Then we would go home and have the stuff for our dinner. I also loved it when we would play "hamburger stand" in the kitchen. We would put the ironing board up across the kitchen (this was the ordering counter). You and the girls were the workers and mom and the boys were the customers. Buttons were the money. That was so fun to me.*

*I remember a few emotional FHE when we were teenagers. It must have been fun for you as parents to deal with so many teenagers at once. I remember having a discussion about a dance at the high school. Mom said I would have to sew a dress for the dance. I came back with "I guess Devin will be sewing his tuxedo then". I can't remember what happened then, but it felt nice to be able to express my feelings and frustrations. In general I remember that FHE was just a natural part of life. Monday was family night and it always was. Just the way church was always on Sunday. I know it was inconvenient sometimes when we were teenagers, but it seems like we all generally were there.*

*One favorite memory is our family theme song "Put your Shoulder to the Wheel". Did we sing it every time? It seems like we did. I like it whenever we sing that song in church now.*

*You and mom did a great job with FHE. I remember it all with fondness.*
*I hope my kids will feel the same someday.*
*Love—Knewie*

Another wrote:
*Dear Dad,*

*I have so much to say about my memories of FHE. However, I honestly don't remember much of them before my teen years—just that we always had it and that I didn't even know any other way. It was never an "option" in my mind. My memories come from when many of the older kids weren't even at home any more.*

*So as a teenager, I can remember not wanting to "come to FHE." I always went thinking that I don't have time for this... BUT I ALWAYS enjoyed it once I was there.*

*I must say too, though, that I well remember Monday night being MASH on TV night. As a teen, I could think "Well, I don't have much time, but I know we will be done at 8:00 so that Mom can watch MASH. I like the way you kept it short while actually teaching us something wonderful. I was grateful that Mom gave us an "OUT" time.*

*Speaking of her, I remember the times that she would laugh uncontrollably when asked to give the prayer. I liked seeing her as silly.*

*Although my detailed memories of FHE are hard to capture, I truly feel that the example you set stayed with me until this day. I feel that FHE should be relaxed and short and simple and not really well prepared either—kind of spontaneous in a way.*

*Today, I know my kids are still young, but they love FHE and they never want to leave the room after because it ends up being a time when we are just hanging out and chatting about different things. I'm sure with teenagers that was not an easy task, but I'm so glad you didn't give up.*

*Love and Thanks, Sarah*

I could give so many other accounts of how our obedience brought us the blessings of heaven. As the priesthood leader in your family, your greatest desire will be to obey all the commandments and promptings that come to you from the Lord. Marilyn and I are so glad that our family life has had a rock hard, immovable foundation made up of our obedience to our temple covenants. Through these covenants, I could lead my family down the path of life for I always knew the direction we should go. By leading them along that path, with obedience, I was truly on a path that would help our family achieve our destiny and help me to eventually become a Fine Old High Priest.

# CHAPTER 11
## KEEPING COVENANTS WILL BRING BLESSINGS

Keeping your covenants will require that you and your wife will often have the opportunity to make sacrifices. Jesus Christ was the great sacrifice. He gave his life for us. The two of you are also asked to make sacrifices. You will likely make your sacrifices not by dying, but by living lives of sacrifice. You will make sacrifices for each other and for the children and for the neighbors and for the Church.

You will constantly look to see who you could encourage, and love. Others could make it along the path if you included them in your love. To reach out to others, you have to go out of your way, even when it is not convenient to do so; that is sacrifice. There will come a time when you will likely be asked to make great sacrifices for the Lord, and you will. You will know the joy that can only come through the feelings that follow sacrifice.

I remember the night when Marilyn really fell deeply in love with me.

I was going to school at BYU. Marilyn and Matt, our young son, had gone to see my parents at their home in American Fork. We were planning to go up the canyon that evening to have a picnic with my mom and dad. Just like the picnics that I had with mom and dad and the family when I was a youngster. We would have hamburgers and olives and potato chips and orange soda.

After school, as I drove through Orem, I saw a family standing alongside the road. They had three young children. I felt impressed to stop. As I talked to them, I learned that they were trying to get to California. I told them I could take them a few miles.

As we rode along we talked. They were a delightful family. The father told me, "Our oldest son is blind. He can't see a thing."

The boy spoke up from the back seat and announced, "I can't see, but I can love."

I swerved a little as I turned back to see such a boy. I loved them so much that I wanted to take them all the way to California, but I couldn't. I let them out in American Fork. As I said good bye, I reached in my pocket and took out a twenty dollar bill. It was the only money that Marilyn and I had to last us for a week. They took the money gladly, and my heart was as full as my pocket book was empty.

At the picnic up at the Hanging Rock campground, I stood by the river with Marilyn and told her of the family I had met and what the boy had said about his being able to love. It took all the courage I could muster to tell her, "I gave them the twenty dollars that you told me to take this morning in case I needed it for something."

When I told her this story, she squeezed my hand tightly. I looked into her eyes and she told me she loved me. That was the night she really fell in love with me. Sacrifice brings many blessings, but none greater than the love that it brings to a family.

It seems that the only way to go further along life's path is to take the time to help others get on the path. Many people could get up and get going if you took the time to encourage them, and to love them. You won't be able to help them all the way, but you can help them take some difficult first steps. But that will require sacrifice.

## THE GOSPEL IS THE PATH

You and your wife have covenanted to live the principles of the Gospel. You will live a life wherein you will honor sacred things. However, you will still have fun. If you don't have fun no one will like you. If they don't like you they will not want you to try to help them. However, your kind of fun will be the kind of fun in which everyone wants to be part, the kind of fun where no one gets hurt. In your fun, you will never make light of sacred things. You will always remember that the most sacred thing is another person.

Another sacred thing is the power you have in marriage to express love and create life. The world makes light of this power. You never will. You will hold these intimate matters sacred.

## TRUST KEEPS THE FAMILY UNITED IN THE JOURNEY ALONG THE PATH

You will forever live the law of chastity. For you the law of chastity, in a very real sense, will be the law of "cherish." The very thought of your wife will bring you a surge of joy and it will be the same for her when she thinks of you. I invite you to see in your mind a vision:

You and your wife are in your house with each other and with your children. Standing outside the house, guarding the family, is the law of chastity. It will not allow anything to enter the home and family that could destroy that trust, for your love is based on that trust.

## IT IS IN GIVING THAT YOU RECEIVE

The two of you promised, when you were endowed, that you would give your all to the Lord. He in turn promised you that He would give His all to you. He endows you with all that He has. An endowment is a gift that, through time, keeps getting larger. Your endowment from the Lord will become ever larger until sometime in the future, when you have made your way completely along the path; you will, as He promised you in the temple, be in his royal courts on high and you will inherit all that He has.

So in keeping with your promise, your covenant to give your all, you will serve in the Church. You will often be over at the church. Your wife will say, "Boy! He sure is over to the

Church a lot. However I knew he would be when I married him. Plus, I have made quite a bit of him since we got married."

There will come a time when you will come home a bit late from your duties over at church. You will be late because someone else wanted to see you. Your wife will have just baked an apple pie that she bought over at the grocery store. She wants it to be hot when you get home so that when you put your ice cream on it will melt down through the hot apples.

Why will she do all of that for you? She will do all of that because you are her hero. She loves you because you are a priesthood man. As you enter the house your children will surround you. It is worth going to a meeting just for the joy of coming home to the family. You will try to eat your pie, but your children will be trying to get some. Your wife will say, "You children leave your father's pie alone. You've already had yours."

And you will reply, "The children can have all my pie if they want." That is just the way it is in a family where all the selfishness of the father goes out the window.

It is sacred family moments such as these that give you an opportunity to teach your children. As you sit together in the kitchen, you ask them where they want to go on a mission and what temple they want to be married in. You will thank them for not cheating in school or anywhere else. In other words, in such a sacred family setting, you can transplant what is in your heart into the hearts of the children. It happens best when the Spirit of the Lord is there because you have been making sacrifices, keeping your covenants and being nice. It will happen a lot in your home.

Now in our exciting story, your wife is at an evening Relief Society meeting. You are at home with the children. You're not sure that you will make it through the evening. However, you finally do. Then appearing in the doorway will be your bride. Not only is she her beautiful self, but she is smiling. She is smiling because she is happy, and there is no greater blessing for a man than that of being married to a happy woman.

Her happiness is so often in your mighty priesthood hands. If I know you, she will be the happiest woman in the town.

## GO FORWARD INTO YOUR BLESSINGS

That is what I would tell you and your eternal partner to remember about your endowment and eternal marriage in the Holy Temple. Remember that just as the footings must connect our house to the earth, so the footings of our priesthood leadership must be Jesus Christ. It is He who connects us to our eternal destiny. Just as He must be the chief cornerstone for the Church, even so He must be the chief cornerstone of your family.

When the foundation is laid upon Him and by Him, that foundation is composed of the principles, ordinances and covenants of the temple. Ignore this foundation and you could still succeed as a husband and father. Without going to the temple, or by not nurturing your temple covenants, you can still provide many windows for your wife and children to see through, and many doors for them to go through. However, there will be something missing, something that goes far beyond shelter, comfort, convenience, personal development, success, fun, and amusement. Something will be missing that has eternal significance something that can only be known by those who have experienced it. That glorious something is the foundation of a priesthood centered home. A home in which the father is a priesthood man and the priesthood leader of the family.

These holy matters that we have just reviewed will forever be the foundation of your priesthood leadership in your family, and you will lead your family along the eternal path to celestial glory.

# CHAPTER 12
## Making Good On Your Promises

Making covenants in the temple will be the foundation of your decision to be the priesthood leader in your home. Obeying those covenants will bring the blessings of heaven to you and your family.

### The Foundation Of A House Is But The Beginning

When Marilyn and I built our house we went to the local government and told them of our plans to build a home. They gave us a building permit. As we began our home we knew the importance of the foundation. The big hole was dug, and the cement for the footings was poured and hardened. The wooden forms for the foundation were then placed upon the footings and the cement was poured into these forms. A few days later the forms were removed.

What if we had stopped there? After all, the foundation is the most basic part of a home. We could have pitched a tent down at the bottom and we would not have had the expense of the plumbing, the electricity, the walls, the floors, the ceilings, the furnace, the closets, the cabinets, the paint, and the carpets. Living in the foundation would have saved us much effort. Somehow we knew if we did that, something would be missing. Plus I think the building inspector might have been a bit upset for our disobedience to the city building codes.

### The Temple Is The Foundation Of Our Spiritual House

In life we are building a spiritual house. We go to our priesthood leaders and tell them of the spiritual home we desire to build. These leaders give us a spiritual building permit, a temple recommend. We joyfully attend the temple to be married. Our loved ones are there. They rejoice with us in our decision to build our spiritual house the Lord's way. We rejoice that we have received our temple endowment and our temple marriage. We know we have the foundation of our spiritual home.

## FOREVER BUILDING

We can't stop there. In the days and weeks and years that go by, we cannot disregard and ignore, to any degree, what we committed to do when we made our temple covenants. If we don't obey our temple promises it will be as though we decided to just stop building our spiritual home. Instead of a spiritual mansion we will be destined to live in a spiritual tent.

## COMMITTING TO KEEP OUR COVENANTS

I painted this picture of my brother John.(Pg. 75)

John is my hero. He is wearing two medals: the Silver Star, and the Purple Heart. John served in the Marines during World War II. On Bougainville and then in Guam he fought valiantly against the enemy. Though wounded himself in hand to hand combat, he carried two of his wounded buddies back through enemy positions to where these men could receive medical attention. It wasn't until the others had been treated that John revealed that he had been stabbed in the leg and had shrapnel from a hand grenade in the side of his head.

For his bravery and willingness to sacrifice his own life to save others, John was awarded the second highest medal that can be given, The Silver Star. And for his wounds he was given the Purple Heart. When our family was told of John's bravery, I was the proudest and happiest little eleven-year-old boy who had ever lived. My brother John was my hero.

John came home and married a movie star looking girl named Wanda. Wanda was my favorite. She taught me how to drive. I loved Wanda dearly. John and Wanda determined early in their marriage that she would be baptized. John was ordained

Painting By George Durrant, of his brother John. Mentioned on page 74.

an Elder. They wanted to have the blessings of being active in the Church but it didn't quite happen. They stopped attending church and for the next 60 years, church was only a small part of their lives. John and Wanda and their three wonderful children loved and were loved. They had very productive lives, but they were of such a nature that all invitations to return to the Church were rebuffed.

Gradually all of my other six brothers and sisters died except John and me. I longed for Wanda and John to come back to church, but I was fearful that if I invited them to do so it could damage my relationship with them. One day, prompted by the Lord, I decided to give it a try. I wrote them a letter inviting them to prepare themselves to attend the temple. I took the letter to their door, handed it to John, and then almost ran back to my car. For the next week I prayed that they would accept the invitation that I had made or at least would not be upset at me for what I had asked them to do. The next week, I humbly knocked at their door. John's greeting was cordial. For the next several minutes, we talked of gardens and weather. Then John looked at me and asked, "Just what would Wanda and I have to do to be able to go to the temple?" I was thrilled beyond measure. The next week John and Wanda were in church.

During the following weeks, I taught them the basic gospel principles they would need to follow to go to the temple. Both of them were surprisingly well informed on these matters. They agreed to do whatever it would take. But then there was a bit of a set back. John announced that he did not want to hurry himself into the temple. He wanted a year to prepare himself for something so important. Wanda felt the same. At first I was disappointed. But then, considering John's deep feelings about personal integrity, I liked the idea of them waiting. John understood what he would commit to do in the temple. He did not want to go there until he had proven to himself that he could be true to the covenants that he would make.

Time has gone by and the year of waiting is nearly over. They have given up their coffee. They pay their tithing. Wanda said that John has changed. He is kinder and more patient. When I go to their home each week it is, for me, like being in heaven. Now, John is even more my hero than he was when I was a young boy. I would like to give him a spiritual Silver Star for his decision to change his life and to prepare himself to go to the temple with his sweetheart, Wanda. They love each other and they long to be together forever.

True, it would have been better if John and Wanda had gone to the temple earlier in their lives, but there is still much to do. What John and Wanda do now, as they go to the temple to receive their endowments and their temple marriage, will enable them to be together here in this life, in the spirit world, at the resurrection, and on into the Celestial Kingdom. There is still much time, even an eternity for John to be the priesthood leader in his home. Maybe John and Wanda could teach us all a lesson that we must not take our temple commitments lightly. We need to be certain that after going to the temple, we will not stop building and thus live in a spiritual tent. Instead we will go on to build and build until we finally have our spiritual mansion.

# CHAPTER 13
## You Will Always Remember

I recall being at the funeral of President Nathan Eldon Tanner. He was once a great priesthood leader in the Church and he became a counselor in the First Presidency. He was also a wonderful priesthood leader in his home. Many of his most inspiring talks were about his family life. His children and grandchildren revered him as a husband, father, grandfather and a fine old high priest. Much was said about this great man's integrity in business, in the Church and in his family. As I sat in the balcony of the Tabernacle on Temple Square watching them move his casket out the side door, I felt a desire to be like him. I wanted to have integrity. I felt that the greatest quality of a fine old high priest is his integrity. And the highest form of integrity is keeping your temple covenants.

### Your Temple Garment Will Remind You To Have Spiritual Integrity

The garment which you first wore as you were endowed in the temple will be a daily reminder to keep your temple covenants and will help you stay on the path that will lead you back to our Heavenly Father. The temple garment will help you to always have spiritual integrity. And spiritual integrity is the very heart of priesthood leadership in the family.

### Experiences While in the Military

I recall a time, more than fifty years ago, when I was drafted into the United States Army. I was at that time married and we were expecting our first child. Back then, the temple garment was top and bottom underclothing sewn together as one garment. It was not two pieces as is most often the case today. For that reason it was difficult to dress and undress in the barracks and the shower room without drawing the attention of the other men to your different underclothing.

Therefore, the direction of Church leaders was that a military man need not wear the garment while serving in the Armed Forces, but he could wear it if he felt he could do so without being ridiculed. When I considered my relationship with the Lord and the feelings I had about Marilyn and our son, I decided I could not bear what lay ahead without the spiritual comfort of the garment. I felt I could always be close in my heart to my family and the Lord if I wore the garment. So I decided to wear it. I knew it would be difficult, however, to me, it would be worth it. Wearing these sacred emblems would give me strength. So I wore it.

During basic training where there is almost no privacy I wore it. I prayed to the Lord that he would support me in this sacred decision. I promised Him that I would never do anything to dishonor or show any disregard for the sacredness of this clothing. I would seek opportunities to dress and undress at times and in places where it would be least likely that someone could see me. I got so I could take my shirt and trousers off really fast and jump into my cot so that there would be little time for others to stare. Of course some still noticed and wondered, but they said little. Once in awhile someone would ask, "What are those?"

I would smile and say, "They are sacred." They didn't ask more.

To shower I could remove the garment in a rapid manner that made it so that others could scarcely see that I wore anything other than what they wore. So it worked out and the blessings flowed.

For example, when we'd be marching I'd try very hard to not make any mistakes, because we had a real mean sergeant. If you made a mistake while you were marching and went right, when you were supposed to go left, he would call you bad names. I didn't want to be called bad names because I did not want to bring dishonor to my priesthood.

Each night when I'd pray, I'd ask the Lord to help me do things right in my training so the Sergeant will not shout profanities at me the way he did at others.

Then one Saturday we were standing in formation in front of our barracks, waiting to be dismissed. I was very happy that we would have the afternoon off, and I was thinking about that instead of about marching. The sergeant shouted, "Left face!"

I got confused and did a right face, and that made it so everyone else was facing away from the sergeant but I was standing face-to-face with him.

My heart pounded with fear, for now I knew that he would look into my eyes and call me names that would be filled with profanities.

But as I looked into the sergeant's eyes, he couldn't seem to even talk. Then in a really soft voice he said, "Private Durrant, turn around." Then he said, "Company dismissed!"

Everybody shouted with happiness and ran toward the barracks. But instead of running and shouting, I quietly and slowly walked away. I was very happy that Heavenly Father would not allow the sergeant to disgrace me.

I feel the garment that I wore made that so.

After basic training and radio school, I was assigned to do a tour of duty in Korea. That meant I would have to leave Marilyn and little Matt. I was heartbroken to know I would be away from them for more than a year. The night before I left Marilyn literally soaked her pillow with her tears.

## Far A Way But Always Close To Home

I went to Fort Lewis to await my journey to Korea. Before I left, Marilyn and I learned that little Matt needed an operation. It was scheduled to be done a week after I was to depart. I called a missionary companion and we gave the little child a blessing that the operation would go well and that Matt would recover quickly. As the days went by, my faith wavered and I was heartbroken to be gone when my little son would need me the most. While at Fort Lewis, Marilyn wrote me a letter. I took the unopened letter to a grove of pine trees down the road a mile or so from our barracks. There I opened the letter and read:

*Dear George,*

*I took little Matt for the operation, however, the doctor looked at his physical problem and said, "This little boy has healed himself. There is no need to operate!"*

When I read that, I lowered the letter and I looked up through the pines and in my heart I heard the words, "Now George, you go to Korea and serve. While you are gone I will take care of your family."

There in that grove of green trees, where I was alone with my God, my heart filled with joy and my attitude and feelings about going to Korea were changed. I knew all would be well.

Many nights in Korea I would go to a private place near the top of a small hill. There I would pray, it was as if Marilyn and little Matt were right there at my side.

## A SACRED EXPERIENCE IN A SMALL BARRACKS IN KOREA

After being in Korea for six months I learned that our base was forming a basketball team, and that the next week they would hold tryouts. Before my mission I had played a lot of basketball, so I decided to tryout. I had sort of lost the touch, but I tried hard and asked the Lord to help me, and He did. I made the team. So my job in the Army became that of being a basketball player. The various units on the base did not feel they wanted useless basketball players in their barracks. Thus we ten men on the team had no place to live. So we built a little bedroom down in the corner of the gym. It was a small room, but it had room for five double bunks and we finally had a place of our own. Not much privacy, but that was all right. There in that little room I continued my, now quite expert, rapid dressing and undressing.

We ten men on the team became dear friends. Each night we would prepare for bed and I, still wearing my garments, tried to be inconspicuous. But in those close quarters I was sometimes noticed as one wearing different underwear than those the others wore.

From time to time I would be asked, "Hey Durrant, what are those underwear?"

I would laugh and answer, "They are sacred and are part of my religion." I would add, "Some time, when the time is right, I will tell you why I wear this underclothing."

We lived there in that little room for four months. One night as I was preparing for bed, still trying to be unnoticed, one of them said, "Durrant, you told us that someday you would tell us about your underwear. How about now?"

I knew the time was right. I asked them all to quiet down because what I was about to talk about was something sacred. I have never had a more respectful and attentive audience. I began to speak and the Spirit of the Lord filled the entire room and the hearts of each of these wonderful friends.

"Men!" I said, "You all seem interested in why I wear this underclothing. Now seems like the right time to tell you. You all know that when I get home movies of my wife and little boy I ask all of you to watch them with me, and I have asked you if you have ever seen such a cute little guy as my son."

"That is right," they all sort of quietly responded.

I continued, "So I know you know how much that I love Marilyn and little Matt."

Then I asked. "Have any of you ever seen a Mormon Temple?"

Each one said that they had, and each commented on the beauty of these buildings.

I said, "You have only seen the outside of these temples. I have been inside the temple in Salt Lake City. As beautiful as these sacred temples are on the outside, they are even more beautiful on the inside."

"When Marilyn and I were to be married in 1956, we went inside that temple. There in sacred ceremonies, we made covenants and promises that we would always be faithful, that we would give ourselves to the Lord, and that we would forever live the law of chastity and other laws of God. When we had made these promises, we were promised by a servant of God that we, Marilyn and I, would not only be together for this life but for all eternity. We were promised that we, and our children would be together as a family in this life and in Heaven. As part of that sacred ceremony, we were given the privilege of wearing these undergarments, like those you see me wear now.

"These sacred garments constantly remind me of the covenants I made with God on the sacred day of our marriage, and of the promises He made to us that we can be together forever. I miss Marilyn and Matt so much while I'm so far from them. But because of these sacred garments and of that which they remind me, I feel that they are very near to me. I know that I never want to be separated from them again. I know that if I keep my covenants nothing, including death, will ever separate us again. I know that the Church to which I belong is the Lord's way. He wants us to be together forever. He wants us to be in Heaven with Him and with our family. I know that this is true and that is why I wear these garments. They remind me to be ever faithful to my family and to my God."

On that sacred occasion when I spoke those words, there was a reverent silence. That little bedroom, in a gymnasium in Korea, on that night, was like a temple.

After that, when we would prepare to play other teams, in the dressing room one of these strangers would see and ask, "What are those underwear?"

When this happened, one of my biggest teammates, a big, African American fellow from Chicago, would stand in front of me and say, "Those underwear are sacred. You just go about your business and don't you worry about that any more."

## I Had The Whole World In My Hands

Several months later I was on the deck of a troop transport boat headed to the west coast of the USA. I had been seasick, but now the waters were calm and so was my stomach. In a day I would be home and I was coming home clean. In Korea there was much opportunity for sin. Many of the men had been unfaithful to their wives there. But for me, my garments constantly reminded me to stay a stone's throw from temptation, and I did.

As I stood on the deck of the ship, there was music playing on the public address system. Several times I heard words I had never heard before. "He's got the whole world in his hands. He's got the whole world in his hands. He's got the little tiny children in his hands. He's got the little tiny children in his hands."

I didn't know at the time that those words referred to God. I thought that they referred to me because I felt, "I do, I do! I have the whole world in my hands. I've got the whole world in my hands!"

## Back Home Again

The next week I was with Marilyn again. It was so good to be home. I knew first hand what heaven would be like. Now we could begin our lives together. There was much for us to do and with the Lord's help we would do it. I was anxious to take my place as the priesthood leader in my home. The temple garment had protected me so that I could do so.

Honor your priesthood. Honor your covenants. Honor your family. Honor yourself. The garment will help you do that and that will make all the difference in you being a priesthood leader in your home.

# PART III

# THE GOAL IS IN SIGHT

# CHAPTER 14
## You Have Help In Keeping Your Promise

A friend of mine told me recently, "I want to keep my promises to the Lord, and be a priesthood leader in my family, but I just keep going out of focus. I run out of spiritual energy. Why is it so hard?"

When Marilyn and I built our house we had a general contractor, and he had sub-contractors. These people did all the work.

### At Home It Is All Up To You

In building our spiritual mansion, we don't have contractors to help. Sometimes the bishop will help for a while, and then the home teachers come and give us a nudge in the right direction. Good neighbors cheer us on. Friends tell us they understand. Grandparents come and for a while all is well. Soon all these folks go their way and the work is still there. So it seems you have to do all the work, along with your wife, in building your spiritual mansion.

### So Much To Do

You, as the father, have to earn a living. Then you come home and help with matters around the house. You have to be attentive to the needs of your wife. You have to be patient with your children, and spend time with them at ball games and concerts and doing homework. You have to mow the lawn, or shovel the snow. You have to discipline your children when it is needed. You have to teach them. You have to be cheerful and pleasant. You have to encourage others even when you are discouraged. You have to set an example of faith and righteous living. You have to spend energy and effort in your church calling. Etc, etc, etc. I chuckle as I write this. Just writing it makes me feel tired.

## THERE IS A WAY TO DO IT ALL

Of course you can't do all of that. There is no way. Or is there? This story stands in my memory:

Some years ago I was serving as a bishop. At the same time I was working on a Doctorate degree at a university and working a full-time job. My children felt that I was spending too much time away from them. I was under considerable strain, fearing that because of my desire to succeed in so many areas I was failing as a man.

One Sunday evening all the members of my ward had gone home. I had stayed for a while to complete some work. I walked into the chapel to turn off some lights before going home. I felt lonely in the empty chapel. As I stood there I felt that my back would not bear for another day, the burdens that I was carrying. I fell to my knees near the pulpit and cried to the Lord. I told him, as one friend would to another, my deepest concerns. I poured out the feelings of my soul to him and described in detail my seemingly insurmountable tasks. When I had finished I remained on my knees, and as I did I heard Him speak to me in my heart. The answer He gave was all I needed, for He said just three things:

Go forward.

Love your family.

Do your best.

I arose a new man. My burdens had been made light. I'd keep going. I would spend less time on the unimportant things in the ward, and I might not get "A" grades in school, but I'd keep going. I'd do my best and that would be success. Most of all, I'd love my family. Oh how I'd love them. I'd love my wife and I'd tell her so. I'd spend time with my children. I'd do my best.

## THE LORD STEPS IN

So when carrying life's loads, just do your best. Sometimes because you are tired, weak and a bit discouraged you do even less than your best, which in reality is your best. Your spiritual mansion begins to rock; and a few bricks fall and cracks appear and your path seems to be less defined.

It is at times like this that the Lord takes over. Because He is the chief cornerstone of your foundation, He won't let you fall. He steps in and becomes your general contractor. Of course he wants to be paid for His effort. He will negotiate with you about that by asking:

"How much will you pay me for my help?"

You reply, "I'll try to keep my covenants."

"You'll try?" He asks.

"Yes. With all my heart I'll do my best, however, as you know from my past, my best is not too good."

He smiles upon you and says, "Your best is good enough."

He adds, "Now if you'll give me room, I'll do for you and your family all the things that you can't do for yourselves. Better still; I'll enable you to do many of these things for yourself in a way it will not seem like work, but pure pleasure."

For me, because my name is George, it seems the Lord says, "Let George do it." At other times he says. "Step aside George, and I'll do it."

But most often he says, "Let's do it together."

When that happens I feel pure joy. "Let's do it together," is the magnificent secret of leading your family in righteousness and in building your spiritual mansion. In life's journey, you can always know that the Savior is just a few steps ahead, marking the way and clearing the path, and his angels are all around you to bear you up. As you move forward in His name you will be endowed with His power. Then and only then can you be the priesthood leader of your family.

# CHAPTER 15
## SACRIFICING YOURSELF TO BE THE PRIESTHOOD LEADER OF THE FAMILY

When Marilyn and I built a new house, we found that in order to get the home we desired we would have to pay just a bit more than we had intended. As we discussed whether or not we could pay this higher cost, we decided we could if we were willing to make the required sacrifices. In other words, we would need to give up certain other things in order to pay for the house.

We learned in the temple that building the spiritual house we desire for our family would also require much sacrifice. In other words, we would need to give up certain other things in order to pay for this spiritual house.

## OUR PATH MUST LEAD TO OUR MANSION

I often go for a walk. I walk a few blocks to the park, then I walk several blocks along the stream. On the way home, I take a different route that leads to my daughter Marinda's house. When I enter her house, I tell her, "The reason that I come to your house each day is because you built your house right in the middle of my walking path."

As I lead my family along the path the Lord has marked, I always find that Marilyn and I have built our spiritual mansion right in the middle of that path. If we do not make the sacrifices necessary to stay on the Lord's path, we will arrive at a lesser house or perhaps even a tent.

## Giving The Lord And Your Family Your Best Will Require Your Sacrifice

Jesus Christ made the ultimate sacrifice. He gave his life as a sacrifice in order that we could live eternally. We also need to make sacrifices. We probably will not give our life by dying for others. Our sacrifices will be made by the way we give our life to the Lord. Giving our life to Him will require much sacrifice on our part and the greater part as fathers giving our lives to Him, is to give our lives to our families.

## Giving Your All To Making Your Wife Happy

As you lead your family along the path the Lord has set, your greatest sacrifice will be to keep your wife's happiness as your highest priority. Your consideration and concern for her happiness and welfare will always be greater than the concern for yourself. The spiritual mansion you and she are building will be of no worth if she is not safe and secure. If you do not attend to her needs you will find yourself off the path.

## You Will At Times Be Off The Path

I love Marilyn; however, at times I wander off the path the Lord has set. In my frustrations, fatigue, impatience and stress, I sometimes say some unloving things and resort to my immature self. I recall just such a time.

## A Long Night And An Ornery Morning

Some years ago our children had a restless night. Neither Marilyn nor I got much rest that night, but she got a lot less than I did. The next morning I had to go to Salt Lake City early. I decided I'd quietly get out of bed and not awaken Marilyn. I'd just prepare my own breakfast and do everything that needed to be done. As I started to get dressed, I went to get a white shirt but there wasn't one ironed. As I asked myself, "Why hasn't she ironed my shirt?" I wasn't feeling quite as wonderful as I had felt ten minutes before. A little disgruntled, I got a clean shirt and ironed it in the places where you have to iron a shirt if you're going to wear a jacket. I then decided I would make myself some toast. There was no bread. I was upset. "Why isn't there any bread?" I thought to myself, "What does she do all day?"

I decided to make hotcakes. I began by following the recipe, but that was too slow. I decided I knew what things went into hotcakes, so I discarded the recipe. Hurriedly throwing in my ingredients, I mixed them all together. Finally the hotcakes were done and I sat there in a lonely kitchen and started to eat. The first mouthful was terrible and all the others more than matched it. With each bite I became more and more upset until I was almost beside myself with disgust, frustration, and self-pity.

It's no good being upset if you're all alone. It's just a waste of energy. So, if you're going to be upset, you've got to be able to show somebody you're upset. So I banged around. You can really bang around in great style in the morning when others are asleep. I banged around until I knew I'd awakened Marilyn, and then I went into the bedroom for the final part of my act. There was a sliding door on the closet which contained my suit coat, and I knew that if I slid it with great vigor it would hit against the other side and make the last big bang. In case any doubt remained, that would definitely let Marilyn know that I was upset. So I vigorously slid the door across and it banged on the other side. Out of the corner of my eye I saw that Marilyn jumped at the noise. Now I knew she was awake.

I then made a cold and calculated decision that I would really let her know how upset I was. I would just put on my coat and leave without saying good-bye. And that's what I did. That is how I left the house that morning, I who was supposed to be a "priesthood man," a man who everybody at church thought was a fine fellow and all that sort of thing.

At the time I was a branch president and had an office in the nearby chapel. I drove down to that office to get some papers to take to Salt Lake City to my meeting. As I picked up the papers it occurred to me that I should pray, because that's what I did every morning in the office. So I knelt down to pray. As I was praying there was only one thing that I could think about, and that was Marilyn. I ask Heavenly Father to bless her that she would have a happy day. After I asked the Lord for that blessing for her, I couldn't think of anything else to say. As I knelt there speechless, Heavenly Father spoke to me. At least, he put an idea into my mind. He suggested, "Why don't you go home and bless her? You're closer to her than I am."

As I arose from my knees, I knew that in order to bless her I had to do one of the hardest things in the world. I had to give the most difficult speech there is to give. Short as it is, it's terribly hard to deliver. I rehearsed it in my mind and I prayed for the courage to be able to say the words. I went home, and for some reason Marilyn was awake. (Apparently something had awakened her earlier.) As I approached her, I looked into her eyes and I could see the hurt that was there. I took a deep breath and gave the speech. I said, "Marilyn, I'm sorry." Then came the speech that regularly follows the words "I'm sorry" spoken between husbands and wive: "And I love you."

I hurried out of the house again. This time I was a real priesthood man and I was ready to do the Lord's work. And, by the way, Marilyn told me that she did have a happy day.

---

I'll bet you could tell similar stories. There are times when each of us priesthood men gets a bit tired of leading our family and building a spiritual mansion. In our immaturity, we say to ourselves, "What about me? I have needs too. If I give my all to my wife and children what do I have left for myself?"

## THEN GET BACK ON THE PATH

It's all right to feel that way on occasion and perhaps take a time out. Put others' needs aside and do something just for you, but then come to yourself and come back home. Come back to your role as the priesthood leader in your home. Repent in the name of Jesus Christ and come back and take your rightful place. You can do it. In the name of Jesus Christ you can do it.

You have been endowed with the power to make the sacrifice of forgetting yourself and going to work for others, and for your family.

You are not perfect in all you do; however you can be perfect in your desire, and with that perfect desire, the Lord will take you by the hand and give you an answer to your prayer to be a good husband and father and to lead your family in righteousness. So don't get down on yourself in spiritual matters and don't default your leadership to society, or to your wife. Hang in there on both your good days and your bad ones. I'll hang in there also, and in our own imperfect ways we priesthood men will lead our families along the path the Lord has marked, and the path that will lead us to our mansion on high.

## YOUR WIFE WILL SENSE YOUR SACRIFICE AND SHE WILL PRAISE YOU

I was told that many years ago one of our past Church Presidents, while speaking in the temple to a group of General Authorities said, "There is much forgiveness behind each one of us being here."

I don't know why, but that story means so very much to me. I suppose it is because that message gives me hope in regards to my role as the priesthood leader in my family. I dream of having Marilyn tell her friends, "George tries so hard to do his duty in the church. However, he saves his best self for me and the children at home."

She could say that except for those moments like that morning which I described earlier. I hope Marilyn, in a forgiving mood could say, "By the way that George treats me in every circumstance, I can say that I know he is truly a righteous priesthood leader in our relationship." I know that in order for her to say, that, there would have to be an abundance of forgiveness behind her words. However on most days, I believe she could say, "I know that George's greatest desire is to treat me perfectly in every way. He can't quite always pull it off, but I know he tries and that is all I ask."

So dear priesthood men, let's you and I try, try, try to treat our wives with love and respect. Let's always try to show that love by the way we treat these glorious ladies in the privacy of our own home. We will never feel better than when we are trying to love and honor our wives above all else, and we will never feel worse than when we fall short. However we will never fall short when we ask the Lord to forgive us and to renew our power to do better in the glorious cause of showing our wife our love by our word and deed.

## RENEW THE COVENANTS OF YOUR TEMPLE MARRIAGE

As a sealer in the temple, I see many couples come to the temple to act as proxies for those who never had the opportunity for an eternal marriage while they lived on earth. In each sealing session, as the session progresses, I see these couples begin to sit closer to each other and to hold hands more tightly as they participate in these sacred marriage ceremonies.

As they hear again the covenants they made when they were married, they feel the sweetness of the Spirit of the Lord telling them to love each other. They sense the eternal nature of their relationship. I've seen enough to know that these couples fall more in love while they are engaged in this sacred work. They go home more resolved to keep their temple covenants and blessings as their highest priority. Through these sacred experiences they are given added strength to put first things first.

Go to the temple. Go there with your wife. Go as often as you can and when it seems wise, go to the sealing room and kneel across the alter from your wife, and renew those supernal covenants you made when you were first married there. I have come to the conclusion that a sealing experience with your wife at the temple has a far greater impact on the relationship between the two of you than would a session with a marriage counselor.

## LOVE HER, LOVE HER, LOVE HER

The sweetest of all the fruits of the Spirit is to feel more inclined to treat your wife as a queen. The most important thing you can do is to keep the happiness and well being of your wife as your highest priority. No sports event, no hobby, no games of any kind should take you away from her. She deserves the very best, so let that be your life long goal to give her the best by being with her and love, love, loving her. The best thing about sacrifice is the feeling that comes with giving yourself to others, especially to your eternal wife and companion.

# CHAPTER 16
## You Can Do It

|———————————————————————————|

Some years ago, while pursuing a graduate degree, I conducted a study on the subject of family home evening and its influence on children. To carry out the research, I located a number of families who had seldom, if ever, held family home evenings. I visited these families, who were less active in the Church, and asked them if they would conduct a family home evening each week for a period of three months. I advised them that I felt that by doing so it would help their children have more self-confidence. To measure the effects of the home evenings on the children, I asked the parents for permission to give their children a "self-image test" both before and after the three months.

### A Reluctant Husband And Father

One man didn't seem enthusiastic at all about my request. He attempted to escape involvement by saying, with some embarrassment, "I can't teach." I assured him that if he would call the family together and do his best, the teaching part would work out all right. I think he only agreed because he lacked the courage to tell me he wouldn't do it. As I left his house, he had little to say and I felt he wished that I had never called on him.

Three months later, I returned, by appointment, to call on him and his family. As I left my car and closed the door, his front door opened and he came out onto the well-lit porch to greet me. I've never met a friendlier man or experienced a warmer welcome.

He immediately called his family of five children together. He, his wife, and the children sat on a stone bench that ran from the fireplace to the other side of the room. I took a seat in front of them and after some conversation I asked the father for a report. The children, ranging in age from teenagers to five years old, burst in before he could respond, and each one expressed enthusiasm for what had happened in the family home evenings.

Then the wife spoke. "It has been a wonderful experience for us," she said, and then with considerable emotion she added, "and the very best lessons we had were those Jerry taught."

I thought that Jerry was one of the children. I smiled and said, "That's quite a compliment for you, Jerry." I then asked, "Now, which one of you children is Jerry?"

The wife quickly replied, "Oh no, Jerry isn't one of the children; Jerry is my husband."

I was a bit embarrassed at my error and my eyes quickly focused on the father. He was looking down, and for a time he remained silent. In a quiet and humble tone he said, "Aw, I didn't do so good."

His wife was forceful and sincere as she replied, "Jerry, when you taught us it just seemed so powerful. It just seemed as if we were a family. We'll never forget the things you said."

Jerry was deeply touched by these heartfelt words. He looked up into my eyes and replied, "I guess I did do pretty good." After a pause he said, "You know, I've always been kind of the black sheep of my family. Growing up, I felt that the others in the family were better than me. So I guess I sort of rebelled and didn't do much in the Church. I got so I just didn't even go."

I listened intently as he continued. "I didn't want to have these family home evenings because I knew they were part of the Church, and besides, I just didn't feel I could do it. But one night after my wife had taught a lesson one week and my daughter another week, I decided I'd try one."

His eyes grew moist as he said, "I'll never forget the feeling I had in my heart as I talked about good things with my family. It just seemed that I was, for the first time, the father that I was supposed to be. I felt so good about what I'd done that the next Sunday morning I decided to go over to the church. I've been going over there every Sunday since then and I've never been so happy in all my life."

Being a priesthood leader to the family does not mean that you have to be Superman. You can do it. All you have to do is...

## Be Pleasant

Don't be ornery. I know a man who, when he came home, stood at the door to his house and uttered a prayer:

"Dear God, I'm sure there is a lot going on inside the house and some of it is nerve-racking to my wife. Please let me go inside and not make matters worse, but instead help me to make things better." Then he'd go in and do it. Help cook, help clean, help create good humor, help make things fun.

You can do that. The Lord will answer your prayers and endow you with the power to be in a pleasant mood, and that is what it takes to be a priesthood leader. You can do that. You'll like doing that better than reading the newspaper or watching TV.

## Have Integrity

Keep your commitments. Keep your temple covenants. That is what it takes to be a priesthood leader. You can do that.

## Be Selfless

This is a bit harder. It will require many sacrifices on your part. But with the Lord's help you will have the power to put your wife in line in front of you. And that is what it takes to be a priesthood leader. You can do that.

Gary Anderson taught with me at BYU. He always got to work earlier than others even though he rode a bike from Orem to BYU. He would get up in the morning and take a cold shower so as to preserve the warm water for his children. Foolish? I think not. His priesthood feelings kept him warm. He rode a bike so the family could have the one family car, an older car at that. Why? Because Gary Anderson was a priesthood man

Boyd Beagle was home alone with his little three-year-old son. The son was in the sand pile. His nose was running a bit, and the dust and the dirt and the crumbs of a cookie were coated around his mouth and nose. Boyd, seeing this, went in the house and grabbed a cold, hard wash cloth and headed out to clean his boy's face. Then he stopped and went back and put the rag under the tap water until it was warm and clean. Then he massaged some soap into it. Then he went out and gently washed his boy's face. Why? Because Boyd Beagle was a priesthood man.

## BE FAITHFUL TO YOUR WIFE

Be nice to everybody, but don't flirt with anyone except your wife. I had a friend who was faithful to his wife, but when I walked with him down a hall or on a sidewalk, and a pretty woman came towards us, we would both see her, but he would turn around and watch her until she was out of sight. He was still faithful to his wife, but he was less than he might have been if his eyes were for his wife only. That is what it takes to be a priesthood leader. You can do that.

## DON'T BE CRITICAL, NEGATIVE OR SARCASTIC

Never speak evil of the Lord's people. I've never met a sarcastic man who was a true priesthood leader to anyone. He may have the calling but he does not have the power. Avoid the poison of being negative and critical of others. Praise your wife and children. That is what it takes to be a priesthood leader. You can do that.

## BE KIND

Someone said, "When in doubt do the kind thing." That is what it takes to be a priesthood leader. You can do that.

## GIVE YOUR ALL TO THE LORD

That is a big one. You can do it if you are willing and the Lord and your family know you are willing. That is what it takes to be priesthood leader. You can do all these things because the Lord will make up the difference between where you are and where you need to be as a priesthood leader for your family.

## BECOME GOOD AT BEING GOOD

I received an email from my daughter recently. She gave a talk in church, and she sent me a copy of the things that she said. I won't share the whole talk, only the part about Kelly, her husband. Here are her words:

My dad has written a couple of books about various aspects of the Gospel. One time, many years ago, I was typing one of his handwritten manuscripts into my computer. At the time, Kelly and I had only been married a few years.

There was a part of that book where Dad was talking about his three daughters and the great men they had married. He mentioned each son-in-law by name and pointed out the specific talents and abilities each one had. When he got to my handsome and wonderful husband, Kelly, Dad basically wrote:

"Kelly? Well! Kelly is just good at being good."

I didn't know how to take that at the time. I felt bad for Kelly. Was my dad saying that my sweet husband had no talents? How could that be? Had I married a man with no talents? Well, the simple truth is that Kelly felt jilted too. So we joked about it with my dad. We said that Kelly felt badly that he had no talents. The next thing I knew, Dad had amended that part of his book to say: "Kelly was good at being good, and in addition to that, he can tell you anything you want to know about baseball, football, or basketball. Now that's talent!"

Over the years, Kelly has told our children that story, and all of us have laughed and laughed. We all love to tease Kelly who relishes such barbs since he is so 'talented' at teasing us right back.

At these fun family times, as the good humor wanes, I'm always the one to get the attention of all the children by asking for silence and then saying:

"You know, being like your father by 'being good at being good' is the single greatest talent you could ever have." And then I add, "You children should know that I have never met a man who is as 'good at being good' as your father. That inner goodness is the reason that I love him with all my heart, and it is also the very reason that he is such a great man, husband and father."

After that sacred moment of pure truth, we again go back to laughing. We laugh a lot at our house because under Kelly's leadership, all of our family is also good at having fun.

By working together with Jesus Christ you, like Kelly, can be good at being good.

Let me share one more thing from Sarah's talk that contains the message I want to give:

Rachel, our only daughter, had her tenth birthday recently, and Kelly had made a few blunders in preparing her birthday party. He was eager to help, but he just didn't understand what Rachel wanted. During those moments, Rachel would just look at me with eyes that said, "Can you fix it Mom?" She didn't even say it out loud because she didn't want to make her dad feel bad.

So then I "fixed it" since it was her special day and since we girls tend to stick together when the boys in our family don't understand.

After Kelly had made three minor mistakes that we had to correct, Rachel was worried that we had hurt her dad's feelings. She said to me in secret, "Dad wants to help, but he just doesn't know what to do. I feel bad because he tries sooooo hard."

Even just trying to be good can go a long way. Jesus Christ knows that each of us make mistakes, but He also knows when we are trying sooooo hard in leading our family. Then He, like my daughter, steps in and things work out.

## It Will All Work Out

When you desire to build on your temple foundation, and when you desire to lead your family along a difficult path, the Lord takes us by the hand and enables you to be good at being good and your grade, as a priesthood leader in the family, will become an "A+."

# CHAPTER 17
## CONFESSIONS AND JOYS OF A PRIESTHOOD LEADER IN THE FAMILY

Dipping into the feelings of my heart, I will now try to evaluate how I have done as the priesthood leader of my family during the half century of my marriage. To do this, let's imagine I'm in a courtroom on trial. The judge will determine if I have been a good family priesthood leader or a poor one.

### ME ON TRIAL

In my mind this will be my most important judgment:

The judge enters the courtroom and the bailiff shouts, "All arise."

As he enters, the judge looks down at me in a way that makes me nervous. When we are all seated he says, "George D. Durrant, how do you plead, do you give good priesthood leadership to your family or do you not?"

I timidly reply, "I try to."

"That is not what I asked. Do you or don't you?"

"I do at times. Most of the time we have family prayer and family home evening. I try to be pleasant and kind. I usually treat Marilyn well and..."

The judge interrupts and says, "I know you do all that. Let me ask you some questions. "You are married to Marilyn, is that correct?"

"That is correct."

"Is she your highest priority?"

"Yes she is."

"How do you show that?"

"I love her."

"Do you defend her? Do you build her up? Do you praise her in front of the children? Do you praise her in private and in public? Do you take her side?"

"Sometimes I do."

"And other times?"

"Sometimes I fall down on those things. I'll try to do better."

"You have eight children, is that correct?"

"That is correct, Your Honor."

"If I asked them if you are a priesthood leader in the home, what would they answer?"

"I hope they would say that I am."

"Do you spend time with them?"

"I do when I have time."

The judge frowns and then asks, "Do you have heart to heart talks with them about things like moral standards?"

"I'm not so good at that. But they know where we stand as a family on those things and they know I am true to their mother. I've taught them to be morally clean."

"Are you patient with them?"

"Most of the time I am."

"What about the other times?"

"I speak sharply at times, but I try to make it up to them later."

"Are you firm in establishing family standards for them?"

"I do pretty well on that. Marilyn is a bit more firm than I am."

"Really? And you say you have family home evening and family prayer and scripture study?"

"We do. We aren't perfect in that, but we do it."

"Well I think that is all the questions that I have. You seem to be doing some things quite well and in other things you seem quite average. How would you feel if I rated you with a grade of "C?""

"I guess that would be fair, but could I say a few things in my own behalf?"

"Sure, go ahead."

"Judge, I feel like I really am trying to be a good priesthood leader in my home. I want that more than I have ever wanted anything. I have been to the temple. I go there as often as I can. I know the covenants that I have made there and, Judge, I really try to keep them. I love the Lord, Judge. I'm not perfect, but if could be I would be. It breaks my heart when I fall short. When I fail to be the kind of husband Marilyn deserves it hurts me inside. When I'm not attentive enough to her needs or lack patience, or respond negatively it breaks my heart, and I go to her and tell her of my sorrow. I tell her of my love. Oh Judge, I want to be so good to her.

"I spend time with the children. Sometimes I'm too busy or too tired, but most of the time I do things with them. I encourage them. I give them blessings. I keep track of how they are doing in school and in life. Oh sure I could do better. I want to be a dad who they can trust and who they can follow. I have always been there to support and encourage my family to follow the Lord's way. I did not always know how to have the perfect talk about intimate matters with my children. However I was always true to their mother. I always told them of my deep feelings about chastity. I did not always know how to discipline my children; however, I always tried to let them know that we have high standards and morals in our family and I have lived by those standards.

"I feel good in saying that during the half century of my priesthood leadership in my home I have loved Marilyn every moment in the deepest parts of my heart. I have taught my family of my deep convictions about my love for their mother and of my love for my Heavenly Father and His son Jesus Christ. I have taught them of my deep convictions about the truthfulness of the restoration and of the true and living Church."

"Judge, I try to do all I do in the name of Jesus Christ. He knows that and He makes up the difference between what I do and what I want to do. I'll do better, Judge. I promise that."

When I finish, the Judge looks into my eyes and says, "You ought to be a lawyer. That was a really good defense. In the light of what you said, I feel I will change your grade. How would you feel about an "A?""

"Oh, Judge I don't deserve an "A." All I want is for my wife to get an "A" and for my children to get an "A". Thank you, Judge. Next time I'm on trial I will do better. I promise you that."

The bailiff shouts. "All arise." The Judge leaves. Marilyn and my children surround me. They say in unison, "Dad, you got an "A". You are such a Fine Old High Priest."

I feel the Judge changed my grade because he could see my desire. He could see not just what I was but also what I wanted to be. It is the same with you. What do you want to be? Because of Jesus Christ what you want to be is what you will become.

## IN OUTWARD APPEARANCE WE DIFFER

Each of us is different in our surface personality and our outward appearance. Therefore it is difficult for any of us to really know how the next man is doing in the very private matter of being a righteous priesthood leader in the home. Therefore you can't really judge your priesthood leadership in your family by comparing your outward personality to the way you see others. Some priesthood men, maybe even you, are so friendly, so funny, so hard working, so able to express love, so gracious, so humble, so in touch with the youth, so smart, so able to communicate, so talented, so...everything that is good. Perhaps these statements describe you, and then again, maybe they don't.

## THOSE I ADMIRE MOST

I have a great love and admiration for those who are such great examples to all the rest of us. I also have an equal love and admiration for the many who only impress those who know them the very best, usually their family. Those who win little public acclaim, but who quietly stand fast in honesty, purity, devotions and love.

My brother Duane was quite a man. He taught school for forty years. He never wanted to become principal. He was content to be in the classroom with his fifth graders. He taught children, and then through the years he taught their children and their children. In the privacy of his classroom he was a master teacher and in his family he was revered.

He was never elected mayor. Nor did he win any public honors. In the Church he was never a bishop, though he was greatly loved by his fellow ward members. To priesthood leaders he just did not seem to be bishop material. Finally he became seventy years old, too old to be a bishop.

Then a stake president prayed and asked, "Who should be the new bishop of the Sixth Ward?"

The answer he received startled him, for into his mind came the words, "Duane Durrant."

"But he is too old and he has cancer."

"He is the man."

The Lord had seen Duane in the classroom. He had seen him help so many along the way. He had often been in Duane's home. He knew of all those who loved Duane and He loved him too.

So Duane became the bishop, and there has never been a better one! The ward thrived under his loving and wise leadership. Seldom did a ward member pray without saying, "And please, Heavenly Father, bless Bishop Durrant."

Shortly after his release as bishop Duane passed away. Surely a humble man such as him would have just an average sized congregation at his funeral. Not so! The large stake center was overflowing and the honest tributes were very personal and amazing.

I tell the story of Duane because he represents those many wonderful men who are priesthood leaders in their home, but who stay in the background in public. Though they may never become bishop, the Lord knows them and He loves them because He knows of their private and good lives. He knows of all the leaders in the Church there are none as noble as those who lead in the home.

## It Is The Family's Opinion That Counts

I knew a man who was a bit below average in social skills. He was not at all stylish in his dress. He was not so good in grammar skills. He had a wife who was a perfect match for him. They had several good children who became impressive in their public lives. I recall this humble man's wife bore her testimony. After expressing her gratitude for the Lord's goodness to her family she said:

"I just want to tell you how much I love my husband. I have never known a greater man than him. He is so good to me. He is so honest. He works so hard. Our children love him. He is their hero. He is our strength. He loves the Lord and he teaches us to be the same. I'm so proud of him. I wish every family could have a husband and father like him."

Perhaps some who heard her words said to themselves, "I thought she was married to old Charlie. What she said didn't sound like him at all." Such an opinion would be wrong, because this man was all that she said. He was indeed a priesthood leader in his home, and he was a Fine Old High Priest.

I will never forget the words of a certain missionary. We were in a missionary zone conference and were having a testimony meeting to conclude the day. Many tears were being shed as each of the missionaries bore his or her testimony. This one missionary, who was known for his valor, stood and testified of the Lord and the Restoration. He then looked at me. (I was sitting on the front row where I could look into each missionary's eyes.) For a moment he paused, and he could not seem to continue.

Finally he said, "President Durrant you are a great man. But I want you to know that you are not as great as my father." He then added, "My father is the greatest man who ever lived."

A few months later his father and mother came to pick him up at the end of his mission. I learned then that his father was quite an ordinary man, but I stood in awe of him because in his son's eyes, he was the greatest man who ever lived.

## The Starting Place

I never was a handsome young man, but I did have a fairly pleasing personality. I had a sense of humor and could make others laugh. I had a carefree attitude that helped me socially. That is the way that I was when I received my mission call.

I'll always remember an experience I had in the mission home in Salt Lake City.

I became good friends with Elder Trigger Edwards from Boulder City, Nevada. He and I would kid around a bit and we loved to be together. As a result, we became instant friends. After three days of training, we were told that if we did not want to get sea sick on our way across the ocean to England, we needed to go to a certain drug store, some blocks away, and purchase some sea sick medicine. So we set out on that errand.

As we walked along, we had a good time talking, laughing and looking up at the tall buildings. We got the medicine and were soon back at the mission home. That is when Elder Edwards said something that I shall never forget. He said, "Elder Durrant, I really like you. You are my kind of guy." Then he added, "Promise me that while you are on your mission, you won't change."

In the early part of my mission I thought of this challenge to not change. I had a good mission in England. So much so that at the end of my mission, I felt that I had become the greatest, average missionary England had ever had. But had I met the challenge Elder Edwards had given me "to not change?" I still had a sense of humor. I was still a bit carefree. I had not given up anything that would alter my personality. So in that way I had not changed.

But had I changed in other ways? I loved the gospel more, I had more faith in Jesus Christ, I was more prayerful, I was more dependable, and I was more dedicated. I was more able to be serious, I felt more worthy, and I had more of a desire to succeed. Other than that I was still handsome and maybe even more so (missions do that for you). I still loved to laugh and kid around but somehow, an average missionary like me had found that in the name of the Lord, I could do things and I could succeed.

## WHERE ARE YOU NOW?

What if you don't want to build a gospel centered mansion? You feel a gospel mansion would be too hard to maintain. You want a gospel house but a mansion seems a bit too much for you. When it comes to spiritual matters you feel like a "C" is about where you are. You don't feel worthy. You never have been a spiritually minded man. To lead your family in prayer and scripture study and those sorts of things, just doesn't come easy to you. You are willing to go along, but not to lead. You feel you would be more comfortable sitting in an easy chair in a gospel bungalow with a big screen TV than trying to be a leader in spiritual matters.

Did you know that with just a slight shift you could be a priesthood leader in your home and that you could get the power to lead your family in spiritual and moral matters? You could go to the temple with your wife and regain your foundation, and you could give her and your children the best gift that they could ever have, a father who is their priesthood leader. If the Lord saw that that was your desire He would help you and you would be on your way.

You get the picture. The Lord knows that you have hobbies and that you need to work to support your family. He knows that you feel weak spiritually. If you will commit yourself to being a priesthood leader in the home, He will make it so that you can do it. He will bless you, and perhaps He will even help your favorite sports team. Maybe He will even help you shoot a lower score in golf and catch a bigger fish. You will never know until you try it.

He can help you have a better attitude when you can't get a bolt loose on your car motor. He will give you energy to climb a higher mountain when you are searching for a bigger buck. He will even help you not to go to sleep in the middle of ESPN's best sports events.

All he asks is that you go to the temple and recommit to your foundation and become a priesthood leader in the home and lead your family down the gospel path. When He sees that the gospel and your family is your first love, then he will make all these other things more meaningful, more fun and more beneficial to your family.

## THE BEGINNING AND THE END

In the beginning of this book I set the stage by quoting a story related to me by my friend, Robert Bryson. Here again is that story:

"While I was at General Conference a few years ago, I walked over to the Relief Society Building. As I approached the room where the displays were, a sister distributing handouts asked me, 'Are you a priesthood leader?' I paused to consider her profound question, and then I replied, 'I believe you would have to ask my wife and children to answer that question. They are the ones who know.'"

## THE ANSWER FROM HIS BEAUTIFUL WIFE DOROTHY

The children and I raise our voice in unison to say, "Our dear husband and father is truly a priesthood man who leads our family in righteousness."

She adds:

I'd like to express what becoming a "priesthood man" does for a "priesthood man's" wife and children. Bob decided early on (probably on his mission) that he wanted to become a "priesthood man", if you will. I could go on for a long time about his priesthood leadership in our home. But just a few things:

With Bob's integrity and brilliant mind he could have easily taken his career to great heights. Instead of working late hours and/or joining business groups and associations, he chose to come home and have dinner with his wife and children every night, and to fulfill his Church responsibilities. Don't misunderstand. Bob had a nice career and was well respected among his peers and colleagues, but clearly in his mind, his career was secondary to family and Church.

Bob has always treated me like a "queen", and made me feel that what I did in the home was far more important than anything he did at work. When he would tell me, "The best part of my day is coming home to you," my heart would soar with love and loyalty for him. He made me want to be a better wife and mother and church member.

When he complimented me for keeping our home neat and orderly, I would find myself cleaning a little harder to please him. When the time came for him to arrive home from the office, I would rally the children to pick up the toys, straighten up the house, set the dinner table and get ready for Dad. When he walked in the door there were a lot of happy hearts there to greet him. We had a happy home.....because he was a "priesthood man".

Our children were likewise affected by this "priesthood man". One day our daughter, Courtney, who was about 13 or 14 years of age said to me, "If Dad told me to cut off all my hair and shave my head I would do it! I would do it because I trust him and I know that he would not ask me to do anything that was wrong." That makes us cry every time we think of that story. Later, that same daughter, upon being diagnosed with MS, called her Dad sobbing and needing his comfort. She reached out to her trusted father in her hour of distress. It was his love and spiritual counsel that brought comfort and solace to her aching heart.

Temple worship always was, and is today, an essential part of our lives, and our children know it. It reminds us of who we really are and what our destiny is. The temple also taught me about the kind of home I wanted to have.....peaceful, orderly, calm, beautiful, spiritual, clean, happy.....are some of the words that come to mind. "Seek ye first the kingdom of God......" has been our "polar star" throughout our lives. It is the safest and surest place to put our trust.

Bob's example has had a lasting effect upon our children and their priorities in life. He has been, and still is, the spiritual leader and patriarch of our home always teaching, always lifting, always blessing, always building and showing the way. A "priesthood man" makes it possible to be an eternal family.

Whenever we have thanked Bob for all he had done for us, he had reminded us, he felt "sacrifice" was too strong a word to describe his feelings about the "cost" or "price" of loving and serving the needs of his wife and family. In his mind, it was the best "deal" or "bargain" he ever made. Of course we were, or so he made us believe.

~Dorothy Bryson

## How Firm A Foundation

Build upon your temple foundation. Rely on the Chief cornerstone, act in the name of Jesus Christ, and follow the promptings of the Holy Spirit. You will be able to do these things and all other things that will bless your family forever.

You may never be perfect at being perfect; however you and your beloved wife and each of your glorious children will be perfect in desire. Then you and your family will, as is promised in the temple, have "power in the priesthood" forever.

# ABOUT THE AUTHOR

George D. Durrant was born in American Fork, Utah. As a young man he was a missionary for The Church of Jesus Christ of Latter-day Saints in England. He received a bachelor of science degree from Brigham Young University in 1956. He also received his graduate degrees, including a doctorate, from the university.

George married Marilyn Burnham, and they had eight children.

George was a professor of religion at Brigham Young University and had been named Professor of the Year and in a student poll was voted as one of the 15 most influential people at the university. He also taught at the church's Institute of Religion in Orem, Utah.

George has been a senior consultant at the Covey Leadership Center.

George has served as mission president of the Kentucky Tennessee Mission from 1972 to 1975, and president of the Missionary Training Center (MTC) in Provo, Utah. He also served a Church Educational System mission to Toronto, Canada.